Pa

Children

and Easy Cakes Too!

Maurice Day

foulsham

LONDON • NEW YORK • TORONTO • SYDNEY

foulsham

Yeovil Road, Slough, Berkshire, SL1 4JH

ISBN 0-572-01580-1

Illustrations by Robert Parry.

Frontcover *Enfants* from Transworld.

Printed in Great Britain by Cox & Wyman Ltd., Reading, Berks.

Contents

Introduction

Is this another party book? Yes, but this one deals with children of the microchip generation. Youngsters who are easily bored — especially by a party based entirely on traditional games and refreshments.

'I told him that's the last party he'll ever have.'

'What went wrong?'

'Everything. They burst all the balloons. Pass the Parcel ended up as a paper war. The battle continued with the sandwiches. And those blow-out squeakers . . . drove me mad.'

Conversations of this sort are all too commonplace amongst mothers of young hosts and hostesses. In this particular case the party guests were eight-year-old boys! Inquiries among other mothers I have spoken to reveal further common difficulties.

'They simply would not join in the games.'

'Turned their noses up at the sandwiches and left me with a fridge full of jelly and ice-cream.'

'One tiny tot bawled her eyes out for her mother and set some of the others off. It was bedlam.'

Not all parties present such problems. Among the thousands I've attended as an entertainer some were delightfully easy for the hostess. They were the ones with small numbers of well-behaved little girls. The majority, alas, are not so easy.

Party giving mothers fondly remember their own birthday parties. The games they played and enjoyed. Those were the days when 'Happy Birthday to You' was sung properly.

Nowadays there are alternative renditions. Youngsters chant, 'Happy birthday to you; squashed tomatoes and stew . . .' Older children finish with, '. . . I saw a fat monkey and I thought it was you.' The final words yelled at the top of their lungs and all fingers pointed at the birthday child.

Today it's a new ball game. To give a successful party you have to know the rules — how to referee the game. Why are children more difficult to entertain now? First, there is a greater freedom — some say lack of discipline. Second, they are used to having constant toys and amusements. Third, television entertainment is fast-paced. Action replays and video tricks maintain interest whenever the action slows down.

Your presentation of party games and refreshments must take these video-age trends into account if you are to be successful.

Elimination games like Musical Chairs are best avoided for children under ten years old. When players are eliminated they can quickly become bored. One distraught lady complained, 'When they were "out" they wandered upstairs and I had a job to round them up for the next game.' To get round this problem it is sometimes possible to change the rules so as to avoid the elimination. Examples are given in the games section.

Long games like Oranges and Lemons are also best left out. Few youngsters have the patience to tolerate the lengthy preamble leading up to the final tug-of-war.

Team games are difficult to referee unless you have plenty of adult helpers. Lines tend to become ragged and cheating will take place unless you have an exceptionally 'good' crowd. However, team games that can be played sitting down are fine.

The author is a children's entertainer by profession, and a member of the Magic Circle. But you don't have to be a professional entertainer to give your child a super party without aggravation to yourself. The secret is in one word. *Planning*.

Have everything you need handy. Know exactly what you are going to do so there are no 'dead spots' between games. This book tells you how.

Act firmly but smile. Look as though you are enjoying yourself — you will infect the children with your enthusiasm and they will be putty in your hands. What about that impossible little horror who insists on trying to spoil everything? There are tips on dealing with him (or her) and other difficult youngsters in the pages that follow. With the confidence that you have more than enough fun and games up your sleeve you can relax and enjoy yourself — and you can be sure that the children will too.

Twelve Steps To
A Successful Party

Helpful Helpers

It is essential to have some help unless you have an exceedingly small group of well-behaved children. Don't have too many helpers though — they'll get in one another's way and may be tempted to sit around and chat. You don't want to strain your voice to overcome background chatter when giving instructions for the games. Two or three friends will be a boon and older brothers or sisters can be supportive. You will be especially glad of any assistance to serve refreshments and see to any mishaps — which usually occur at the most inconvenient times. In the middle of serving melting ice-cream you may hear the cry, 'I want to go to the toilet,' or 'I've spilt my drink.' If you can call on someone else to deal with these problems you will maintain a calmer frame of mind.

Good Timing

Having decided to have a party, you need to set the date. Ask whether any of your child's friends is having a party around the same time. If dates clash, your guest list may be decimated — which may be a good idea if your list is too long, but can also cause considerable upset if children have to choose which party to go to.

It isn't essential to have the party on the actual birthday. Other considerations may make another day a better choice. Midweek may be inconvenient if you have a job and time off is tricky to arrange. On the other hand a midweek party won't interfere with adult weekend activities. Another advantage of weekday parties during school term time is that they start later and are often shorter. Easier for you if you are unsure of your ability as an organiser.

Weekends may allow you more time to prepare, and if you want to go out that evening why not have a lunchtime party for the birthday child? These start at around 11.30 a.m. and end about 2 p.m. This time is better for three and four-year-olds who tend to tire as the day wears on.

Whatever the age group and whenever you hold your party don't make it last too long. Two and a half hours is enough for six-year-olds and upwards. Two hours for three to fives. Remember the old showbiz maxim — leave them wanting more.

How Many Guests?

A dozen or so is ideal for a primary school age party where the children can play lots of games. For younger children it is best to keep the numbers lower. Little children often need individual attention, and if one gets upset it can spread like wildfire.

If your child wants to invite, 'All my class at school, my best friend next door, cousin Jamie . . .' you can easily find that the list totals 45 or more. The solution could be to hire a hall, but you must think carefully about the cost and planning before agreeing to the birthday child's demands. Being in a large hall produces in most children a compulsion to run and yell. Only very careful planning and good control can prevent the party becoming a very expensive free-for-all.

Many people have 'joint' parties. Two, three or four birthday children all invite their friends so that there may be fifty or more guests. By doing this the cost of hiring a hall is shared and parents often find they can afford to hire an entertainer to present games and a magic show.

However many you invite, try to have girls and boys mixed. If your son goes to an all-boys school, try to limit the numbers from his class and include children from relatives and neighbours. This helps to prevent school cliques forming and giving you trouble.

Where To Have Your Party

Church halls are generally cheap to hire. Some hotels, clubs and restaurants have rooms to hire, but may insist that you use their catering service. A few schools are also prepared to accept party bookings.

Do try to use a hall that you know, or that a friend has used. If this is impossible, at least pop along to see the hall before you book it. Some are too large. One cavernous church hall I visited sported a piano and stage complete with props. On arriving to present my hour's magic show I was greeted by a minor riot. Several children were running on to the stage and jumping down to the floor of the hall. Others were playing with the props used by the church amateur dramatic society. Five young would-be musicians pounded the piano. A distraught hostess said, 'Thank goodness you're here. Can you start right away?' She helped me round up the youngsters and I organised them in a quiet game whilst I set up my show.

If booking a hall of this type is unavoidable try to block off the stairway to the stage. If there is a piano turn it so the keyboard is jammed against a wall.

Check you have access to water — you'll need it for the drinks. Tables and chairs should be handy — you'll be expected to pack them away afterwards. If they are stacked in an adjoining room you'll wish you'd booked a removal firm to help you!

In clubs, ask about the lighting. If they have only a few fairy or disco lights you may suffer from eyestrain by the end of the party!

Most children's parties are held at home. Clear as much furniture as necessary from the party area to give room for the games. If you have valuable ornaments it would be prudent to move them out of range. Accidents do happen.

During fine weather it is tempting to have the whole shooting match in the garden. If you have swings, slides or a climbing frame you won't need so many games. But you must be prepared to arbitrate when squabbles break out. 'Jane won't let me have a go on the swing,' 'Jason keeps pushing me down the slide.'

You'll also need to keep a watchful eye open if you have any prized plants.

Do you live on a main road? Traffic noise can deaden your voice and a slight wind can take it in the wrong direction — disconcerting when giving games instructions. You live under a flight path of jets? Forget an outdoor party.

Tempting Invitations

Written invitations are best. Verbal ones can be forgotten or misheard. The time, date and venue are essential pieces of information. Your phone number is also useful. If anyone can't attend, it is easier for them to phone you — they may forget to write, or simply not bother to.

You can buy invitation cards from stationers or make your own. Buy some coloured cartridge paper from an art shop or local printer. Cut it to size and ask the birthday child to help you write the invitations: Please come to my party at 38 Abbotsford Gardens, Woodford Green. It's from 3–5 p.m. on 1st June. Phone 123 4567. You can decorate the cards by adding colourful stickers.

If you don't hear from some of the invited guests, phone a week before the party to check. Then you can invite substitutes or cut down on the refreshments.

If the venue is hard to find, or it's dark at kick-off time, tie a few balloons outside. Arrivals by car or taxi can then locate the party with ease. If there's another bunch of balloons a few doors away, add a notice: 'Marc Smith's party.'

Costumes And Decorations

Balloons are the traditional way of decorating the party room, and can be handed out when the children go home. Try to have them out of reach till the end of the party — lively lads will burst them. Apart from balloons, it is only necessary to make the party food look festive and colourful.

Blowouts with squeakers are best left till the end of the party — or forgotten altogether. If the birthday child insists, give them out at refreshment time. Before you continue with the games after they've eaten, collect the blowouts and put them out of sight. You need strong nerves and a loud voice to direct games during a bout of squeakerism! Party hats can help to provide a colourful scene for the home video but don't force them on unwilling guests. Many girls dislike them because they disarrange their hair and some boys think they're unmanly.

Another idea is the fancy dress party. Again, it makes the video more interesting viewing but there are snags. Some costumes are too elaborate and restrict the wearer when the games are played. Also, you may have a pretty girl who arrives in an Emmanuel-type outfit and is envied by the others. The child whose parents are not so well off may sport a nondescript outfit and feel embarrassed or humiliated. Why not try a 'hat party'? Tell the guests their hats must be home made and represent something or somebody. During the games period they can be removed easily if necessary.

Halloween parties are gaining popularity. Witches' hats and cloaks are cheap to make and are classless. Also they don't restrict the wearer in most of the games.

What Sort Of Refreshments?

Small, novel and varied is the rule for refreshments. Sand-wiches are old hat. They can be made tempting, however, by cutting off the crusts, shaping with pastry cutters and giving them interesting fillings. Banana, meat or fish paste, Marmite, honey and jam are all liked.

The best idea is to present the guests with a wide variety of nibblets like cheese balls, potato rings, pineapple chunks, and crisps. You could also try snacky tasties like stuffed tomatoes, cocktail sausages and vol-au-vents.

For sweet, most children don't go over the moon about jellies. If you add ice-cream, you'll find some don't want jelly, others will refuse the ice-cream, and chaos will result. Try chocolate fingers, Smarties, small iced cakes, chocolate eclairs, funny-face biscuits or arctic roll.

Orange squash and Coke are popular drinks, as are milk shakes provided you don't mind the trouble. However, don't give too wide a choice of drinks because you'll need extra helpers to provide a good service. Some young party-goers love ice-cream in fizzy drinks. Give them a spoon and straw. The same type of refreshments that you would serve at afternoon parties can also be served at lunchtime. But if you want to give them something more appropriate try fish fingers, beans on toast, or sausages and chips as the main course. Alternatively you could buy burgers and chips from the local hamburger bar. The sweet is the same as for afternoon parties.

Wherever you have your party, paper cups, plates and tablecloths save washing-up time. Shovel all the debris into plastic dustbin liners at the end. If you haven't enough space to sit all the children round the table, you can make the meal into a picnic. Lay an old sheet on the floor and cover it with a paper tablecloth. The guests sit on the floor and eat their refreshments out of individual cake boxes. Anything they don't like, they leave in their box. This way you don't have any hassle with fussy children. Have a dishcloth and kitchen roll nearby to wipe sticky fingers or mop up spillages.

It is best to serve refreshments after the children have played some boisterous games. Present a few quieter sitting-down games immediately after they've eaten to prevent upset tummies.

When most of the guests have finished eating and show signs of restlessness, present the birthday cake ceremony. Good bakers sell children's cakes in several interesting designs. Fairyland cottages, football pitches, Superman, Mickey Mouse, trains, Tom and Jerry. If you make your own cake, decorate it with Smarties, chocolate buttons or allsorts. If the birthday child's name isn't too long you can write it on the cake with small sweets. Remember to have matches or a lighter at hand to light the candles. Delay at this stage can be fatal since the children are usually raring to get on with the party after they've eaten.

If there are a few cheeky boys around, keep them away from the cake or you'll be forever re-lighting the candles as they blow them out prematurely. You don't need to serve the cake at this stage — the children will be too full to eat it. Cut slices and wrap them in serviettes to be taken home.

Don't forget tea or a glass of wine for yourself and adult helpers. If the going gets tough it can act as a palliative!

RP

Making Music

An essential ingredient for any party is music. It sets the mood when the guests are arriving and is essential for certain games. You can buy special children's party music on record or tape, but remember that taped music is easier to control in games like Pass the Parcel that require music to continually start and stop.

Music played directly from a radio won't always be lively enough and has too many gaps when the presenter is chatting. Records have silent spots between tunes, which may fall just when you want the music to play. Doesn't taped music suffer from the same snag? Not if you tape suitable music from radio or record so that one tune immediately follows the other. This is easy to do if you have a twin tape deck or an extra tape recorder. First, record a complete programme on tape 1. Then transfer only the wanted parts to tape 2. Thus you eliminate all the unwanted gaps and chat.

Winning Prizes

One of our neighbours held a party for her five-year-old daughter. The girl had an eight-year-old brother who was allowed to invite a couple of his pals to make up the number. Later, the woman told us, 'It nearly ended in disaster. We'd bought some rather expensive prizes and the bigger boys kept winning. Two of the smaller children bawled their heads off and we only averted trouble by banning the older boys from competing.'

Even if all the children are the same age, competitive games can produce the same few winners every time. Some cheating on your behalf can ensure a more even distribution of prizes and a more satisfied group of youngsters. If they are very young it is prudent to have consolation prizes for the losers. You will then avoid the possibility of tears flowing from persistent triers who don't win.

Expensive prizes can encourage the 'collector' who will fight like mad to win. It may also be a good idea to avoid sweets. Publicity in recent years about dental hygiene has encouraged some parents to limit or ban sweets for their children. Also they are commonplace and lack novelty appeal. Small, cheap novelty toys are ideal prizes — necklaces, rings, brooches, pirates' eye patches, pencil-top animals. They can be bought from toy shops or advertisers in catalogues or Exchange and Mart. One firm will supply an assortment of 100 small toys for around £6 at the time of writing. At that rate you can afford to give every child a couple of prizes so nobody goes home disappointed. Always look out for unsuitable items — remember tinies are likely to put things in their mouths.

It is best not to give out prizes at the time they are won. If you do, the recipient will examine his toy, watched by some of the other children, thus disrupting the next game. Also, if the prizewinner loses or breaks his toy he will cause disruption asking you for another one.

The best method is to keep a list of names and put a tick beside the appropriate name when a prize is won. This enables you to keep a check on the winners and helps maintain that equitable spread of prizes. Ask them to line up at the end of the party to collect their winnings and piece of birthday cake. If anyone hasn't won any games tell them, 'You played the games so well I'm going to give you a prize too.' If possible, give all the girls the same prizes and all the boys the same. This will overcome the problem of, 'I don't want this — I want the same as Terry.' Things are confusing enough at the end of the party when parents are calling for their offspring.

If you have the time and inclination, put the prizes in a big box. Cover it with decorative paper and letter the word PRIZES on it. If you have separate prizes for girls and boys divide the box with a piece of card.

The Party Day Arrives

Now you are prepared for the great day. As it approaches ask yourself whether you have forgotten anything. There's a check list on p. 23. You may find it useful to give every child a name badge to wear. These can either be bought or made from card, and enable you to immediately call a guest by name. A boon if that child is misbehaving. The sound of their name will pull them up short and nip any naughtiness in the bud.

If the children are young, make sure they can't lock themselves in the toilet. An older child or an adult can stand guard if you have to remove the key or bolt.

As the guests arrive, to cheerful background music, the birthday child will greet them and receive his presents. Persuade him to leave his presents unopened until the end of the party when everyone has gone home. It saves vital parts being lost or damaged by his friends. And it won't be easy to start games with presents and wrapping paper strewn all over the place.

Coats can be put in another room on a settee or bed. If you have a large number of guests write names on pieces of paper and tuck into coat pockets. It will save confusion at the end.

The most difficult part of a party is when the guests are arriving. You may be lucky enough to have a group who will chat among themselves until games time. Generally this doesn't happen. Each new arrival may be greeted by the others running into the hall chanting, 'Who's at the door . . . who's at the door . . .' Rather disconcerting if you were hoping to organise them into a game. There *are* games that can be played during this awkward time. They must be suitable for varied numbers of players and be capable of surviving interruptions. An up-to-date version of Hunt the Thimble is an example and is described in the games section.

An easier alternative, particularly for younger children, is to let them play with your child's toys — providing there's no objection. When most of the guests have arrived announce that it's game time and ask your helpers to dispose of the toys.

Troubleshooting

Be prepared to deal with troublesome or awkward youngsters. Here are some well-known problems and how to overcome them:

The shy, sensitive child. If they have a friend or acquaintance at the party ask that child to 'look after' the shy one. Don't force them to join in boisterous games — let them watch on the sidelines. Try to encourage them to take part in a quiet, sitting-down game.

The tearful child. Sometimes a sensitive youngster will cling to the parent who brings him to the party. They often cry bitterly at the thought of leaving mummy. Let the parent stay if they wish. If they have to leave, take their phone number in case you are left with an uncontrollable flood of tears. Give the child a toy to play with. If that fails try a sweet. Try to enthuse him with the goodies in store. Still sobbing his heart out? Tell him, 'I'll phone mummy to take you home. She won't be long. Stay with Auntie Ethel and watch for a while.' Another ploy is to usher the tearful one into another room and ask Auntie Ethel to read a story. Usually you will find that these children will settle down and join in the party. In the rare instances when *nothing* will placate the sensitive child, you will have to make that phone call.

Over-keen competitors. In games where you select one child at a time to do something, you could find yourself surrounded with yelling youngsters. 'I want a go,' 'I haven't had a turn,' 'Can I be next?' It isn't fair to choose the one shouting loudest, yet you don't want anarchy upsetting the quieter children. Simply say, 'I'll choose the best one sitting quietly. Ssshhh.' You will quickly restore order and can continue in complete command of the situation.

Troublemakers. Naughty rascals who misbehave must be stopped immediately. You may be unlucky enough to have the school bully at your party. He will want to wrestle with weaker boys and you'll end up with a rough and tumble on the floor. This is where the name tags are useful. Call his name loudly and firmly. Continue, 'No fighting. This is a party and we're here to enjoy ourselves. You won't win any prizes unless you play the games properly.' When he knows he's been rumbled you shouldn't have any further trouble. On the rare occasions when you have a persistent offender tell him that he will go into the 'sin bin' if he misbehaves. He'll look puzzled. Explain that he will be sent into another room and miss a whole game. One of your helpers can go with him and give the little horror a pep talk. If he knows that he won't be allowed to wreak havoc you will usually find he'll co-operate.

Don't be afraid to put your foot down. The children will respect and admire you for curbing the school rascal. They would rather enjoy the party in a controlled manner than engage in a free-for-all.

The accident-prone child. Have some band-aid plasters handy. Other first-aid items could be helpful, so be prepared.

Party Checklist

- [ ] Decide time and venue
- [ ] Confirm any bookings a week before the day
- [ ] Work out a time-table
- [ ] Invitations
- [ ] Games list and props
- [ ] Music
- [ ] Pencil and paper for guest list and prizes check list
- [ ] Name badges
- [ ] Prizes
- [ ] Party hats
- [ ] Balloons and string
- [ ] Refreshments
- [ ] Birthday cake
- [ ] Candles
- [ ] Matches or lighter
- [ ] Paper cups, plates, tablecloth
- [ ] Cake boxes — for a picnic party

☐ Dishcloth & kitchen roll

☐ Plastic bin liner(s)

☐ Adult refreshments

☐ First aid kit

☐ Whistle

☐ Enlist help

Alternative Parties

Entertainers

If you feel you can't cope with running the whole shebang but you still want a fairly conventional party with tea and games, the answer could be to book a children's entertainer for an hour. They advertise in local papers and Yellow Pages and will present a magic show with puppets, ventriloquism, balloon modelling or other novelties. Ask your friends whether they can recommend someone. Failing that, phone several and ask them what they do for the age group who will be at your party. The better ones sound as though they have a pleasing personality to which children can relate. They should also be able to give you a guide to their performances. If an entertainer says he presents fire eating and swallows razor blades for four-year-olds, look elsewhere. There are a few who can run the whole party — games and entertainment. If you engage one of these your only concern is the refreshments. If a professional entertainer is too expensive, read the Conjuring Section (p. 95) and persuade a friend or relative to present a short magic show between games sessions.

If you can't be bothered with the hassle of party games at all, here are some alternatives.

A Restaurant Party

Many fast-food chains cater for children's parties. Some offer to entertain your party guests as well as feed them, and can supply a birthday cake if required. If they cannot offer this additional service you'll have to make the party time shorter than usual. When they've finished eating the guests

25

will run around and be bored if there's nothing organised for them to do.

Some children's entertainers can present a magic show at restaurants like these, which solves the problem of what to do after the food has been eaten. Make sure they are experienced. Many fail to cope with the difficult conditions in some restaurants. They have to compete with noise from staff and customers; Espresso machines; background music. It is also very important to check with the restaurant manager that it is acceptable for you to have an entertainer. Otherwise you could find him being less than helpful over matters such as a conflict between his piped music and your entertainer's voice.

Dozens of pubs have been converted into fast-food out-fits. A few have special equipment to amuse children. For example, ball ponds. Hundreds of plastic balls are enclosed in a large caged area. Youngsters leap into the seething mass from a low platform around the pond. They can have a romp for a while and then settle down to the party tea.

Inflatables

You can hire a huge 'bouncy castle' or similar inflatable for the whole party time. They may be expensive but children love exploring them and bouncing all over them. Ball ponds are also available for hire.

All you need is a reasonable-sized garden. However, there is one snag. If rain is forecast they could cancel your booking. Even if they don't, it won't be much fun.

If you hire an inflatable it is important to have plenty of adult helpers. There may be a few bumps to cope with, and it is essential not to allow the bouncers to get over excited and out of control.

A Sports Party

If you have to cope with a large number of lively boys, try a football or cricket party. All you need is an adult who knows the rules. And who has the authority to apply them fairly and firmly.

If your garden is too small, see if you can hire a school. Some have their own sports ground and may be willing to hire it to you. Any boys who are not interested in playing can act as linesmen or spectators.

Alternatively, for something a little more exciting, you could take a group of youngsters to a local swimming pool, skating rink or sports centre. A lot of these now offer special party rates which may include food, sports tuition or private use of the facilities. If you decide to go on a trip like this, make sure that you know exactly what you will be getting for your money and check, before you book, that the activity is suited to the age group involved. Take enough helpers, preferably people with some experience of the sport involved, and tell the parents of your guests precisely what you will be doing.

Trips And Treats

Trips and outings can make excellent birthday treats for any age group, and to suit any pocket. During school holidays many cinemas show films suitable to younger audiences, and in many areas there are children's theatres too. Local tourist attractions are also well worth thinking about — historic houses, steam museums, wild life parks or even your neighbourhood park and playground. Whatever you decide to do, ask about party rates and check whether you can buy food there or take a picnic. Also, most importantly, make sure the guests know what sort of clothes will be suitable. Nothing makes a child more miserable than arriving at a theatre in jeans or at an adventure playground in a frilly party dress.

Party Plan For An Outing

2.00 p.m. Guests arrive at your house.

2.15 p.m. Leave for party venue. (Have children allocated to cars beforehand, and do not allow *any* changes, or everyone will want to swap around and complete chaos will result).

2.45 p.m. Arrive at party venue and enjoy the swim/skate/roundabouts.

4.00 p.m. Extract children and prepare them for tea.

4.20 p.m. Tea.

4.45 p.m. Finish tea and return to cars.

5.15 p.m. Arrive home for guests to be picked up at 5.30 p.m. (If it is hard to be certain when you will arrive back, you could offer to drop all guests at their own homes, giving each driver a convenient group of addresses, and parents an approximate time of arrival).

RP

Checklist: Trips And Outings

☐ Confirm any bookings a week before the day, including venue and catering.

☐ Finalise travel arrangements; allocate children to cars; check that parents know how you will be travelling.

☐ Divide the guests into groups — one for each helper — and write out the names so that everyone knows exactly who is responsible for whom.

☐ Work out your time-table.

☐ Prepare 'emergency kit' of baby wipes, elastoplast, bin liner, safety pins . . .

☐ Select a few games and songs to get everyone happily through the journeys to and from your destination.

All Sorts Of Games

Don't involve yourself in unsuitable games. Or games with which you are not familiar. Any disputes about the rules must be settled by the referee — that's you. Some games have variations in the rules depending on their author. If a child says, 'We don't play it that way,' you reply firmly, 'No but that's the way we play it in *my* book.' If you involve yourself in a discussion about the rules the hold-up will cause chaos and confusion. The attention span of most young folk has its limitations. If they are waiting around for something to happen they could get up to mischief.

Uninteresting parts of television sports events are covered by action replays and studio interviews. Light entertainment and music programmes maintain a fast pace by the use of video tricks. You can't use these devices, but you must still ensure that there are no dead spots when the children are looking around waiting for something to happen. List your games and play them non-stop. Alternate lively ones with quiet, sitting-down games. Some, like the Farmer's in his Den, can be played several times. When you think they are tiring of the game, change it for another one. Ask your helpers to persuade reluctant children to join in, so that neither you nor the other guests are distracted from the game in progress.

Games To Arrive To

In the excitement and confusion when guests are arriving there are few games that can be played successfully. If the children are happily chatting together you need do nothing. They may, however, be raring to go and will look to you for guidance.

Very young children are happy playing with toys — providing your child doesn't mind lending his precious possessions. Keep your eye open to settle disputes over who should play with what.

Fishing

For older partygoers (nine years plus) make a simple fishing game. Cut some fish from stiff paper. Draw a few scales and eyes with a felt pen. Cut holes at the mouth end and bend upwards — the diagram will make it clear. Fishing lines are made from string or cotton with paper-clip hooks. If you want to go to the trouble, dowelling or knitting needles can be used as rods. Players try to hook a fish. When they catch one they replace it and try another one. You could give a prize for the one who catches most fish, but the important thing about the game is that it gets everyone involved right from the minute they arrive.

Giant Noughts And Crosses

Another game for older children, this is simple, quick and fun. Make a grid from string. Cut out large circles and crosses from magazine paper. You need five of each. The game can be played as many times as you like, and newcomers simply added to the noughts or crosses team as they arrive.

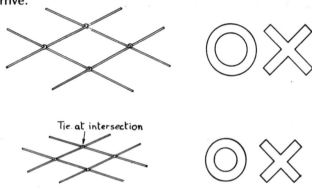

Tie at intersection

Grid for Noughts and Crosses

Five of each of these

Hunt The Thimble

For children aged from five to nine try this version of Hunt the Thimble. It can be played by two or more children and can survive interruptions from arriving guests — ideal as an opening game. You need only a thimble.

Rules: One player hides outside the room. The thimble is placed somewhere in the room. It must be visible — not hidden under anything or placed too high up. When the player comes back into the room the others sing: 'Half a pound of tuppenny rice, half a pound of treacle, that's the way the money goes, pop goes the weasel.' If the player is searching in the wrong place they sing quietly. As he gets nearer the ditty is sung louder and louder. When he finds it he selects another child to hide outside. It is surprising how difficult it is to locate a tiny object that is in full view — even if it is on the middle of the floor. The fact that every child is involved keeps them interested.

Treasure Hunt

For slightly older children a more complicated hunting game works well during the arrivals. Before the party, hide a dozen or so small objects (e.g. sugar lump, safety pin, button etc.) around the room in places where they can be found without anything being touched. Have ready several copies of a list of the hidden objects, and some pencils. It is more fun for the children to play this game in pairs or small groups, rather than individually. As each pair or group arrives, give them a copy of the list, and a pencil. The trick is for them to find all the objects, but not give away their whereabouts to everyone else!

Kipper Race

This amusing game is quite simple to prepare, and like the other games in this section it will get everyone joining in.

1. Cut out six fish shapes from a newspaper or magazine.

2. Attach approximately two metres of thread or string to the mouth of each fish with sticky tape.

3. Tie and tape the other ends of your strings to rolled pages of newspaper or magazines.

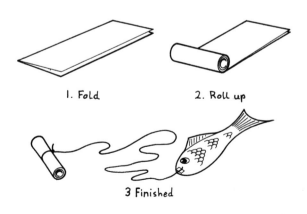

1. Fold   2. Roll up

3 Finished

If you want a deluxe job use lengths of dowelling instead of rolled paper. For the fish, cut from thin card and decorate with coloured pens.

The idea of the game is to turn the rolled paper round and round to 'reel in' the fish. Play it as a race. This game is ideal when only a few guests have arrived, but if you do have more children than fish, the onlookers can be encouraged to cheer until their turn comes around.

Find The Word

This needs a little preparation on the part of the organiser, but it is much enjoyed by older children. It is an excellent game to play while your guests are arriving, since they can easily join in when others are already playing.

Choose a fairly long word in which no letter occurs more than once, such as 'worshipful' or 'laughter'. Write it out in capital letters as many times as you have guests, and then cut each copy into individual letters. While the children are elsewhere, or before they arrive if it is to be the first game of the party, hide all the letters round the room. When the guests come in, tell them that they must find ten different letters (or however many there are in the word you have used), and then make them into a word.

Match The Picture

This game is similar to Find the Word, but can be played by much younger children.

Collect a number of coloured pictures beforehand, old Christmas cards or postcards are ideal, allowing three or four per child. Cut each card in half, and hide one half of each card around the room. As the children arrive, give each one half a card, and tell them that they must find the other half. When a player has successfully completed one picture, they can be given another half, and so on until all your guests have arrived and the party can begin in earnest.

Games For Tinies (3–5 Year-Olds)

Many people have parties for three-year-olds. The age of awareness is lower than it has ever been. However, their attention span is short and many are reluctant to join in organised games. Let them play with a few balloons or toys for a while. Then ask your helpers to remove the toys and try the following games. The first six are quiet games, which should be alternated with the other, more energetic ones.

Alphabet Tower

You need a set of alphabet blocks or building bricks. Ask the players to sit down in a circle. Put a block on the floor in the centre of the circle. Give the next block to one of the children and ask her to put it on top of the first block. Continue round the circle giving the blocks out and asking each player to balance his one on top of the others. If they fall down, start again with the next child. If one of them is hopeless you can guide them. The game can be played several times before they tire of it. Don't overlook it because of its simplicity — that is the keystone to games for tinies.

Nursery Rhymes

A rubber ball and a list of nursery rhymes are the props for this one. The children sit in a circle and pass the ball from one to the other as you play some music. Whoever has the ball when the music stops has to recite a rhyme. You lead the others in miming actions to fit the rhyme. For example: Hey diddle, diddle, the cat and the fiddle (mime playing a violin), the cow jumped over the moon (move your hand in an arc over your head), the little dog laughed to see such fun (say, 'Ha, ha, ha'), and the dish ran away with the spoon (running motion with two fingers). If a child is too shy, ask someone else if they'd like to take her turn. Sometimes they may need a little prompting.

Little Laura

Buy a box of Smarties and you've bought yourself a winner. You also need a plate. Put the plate on the floor and sit the children around it. Place six Smarties on the plate — as many different colours as possible. One tiny tot hides outside the room — let's say her name is Sara. You indicate one of the Smarties and ask the children to pretend it is called Little Laura. Sara is asked to re-enter the room and take the Smarties slowly one at a time from the plate. When she touches the chosen sweet everybody calls out, 'Little Laura.' Sara keeps all the Smarties she's taken including Little Laura.

Make up the number of Smarties on the plate to six and choose another child to hide outside. Select a different colour to be Little Laura and repeat ad lib.

Currant Buns

The players sit down in a group. One is chosen to stand in front of them, say her name is Lisa. They all recite a rhyme and do a simple mime: 'Five currant buns in a baker's shop' (hold up four fingers and a thumb), 'round and fat' (hands go round in a circle), 'with sugar on the top' (hands on heads). 'Along came Lisa with a penny one day' (point to girl), 'bought a currant bun and took it away.'

Lisa then chooses one of the others to join her. They all repeat the rhyme but start with 'Four currant buns'. Another one is chosen by Lisa and they continue with 'Three currant buns'. When they have finished with 'One currant bun' someone else is chosen to take Lisa's place.

The Farmyard

This is an excellent game that is always much enjoyed by very young children. All you need is an adult who can tell a simple story!

The children all sit around the story-teller, who gives each the name of a farmyard animal. If there are a lot of children, it will be all the more realistic to have several cows, sheep, chickens and so on. The story-teller then begins to tell the story of the farmyard — a day on the farm perhaps — and each time one of the farm animals is mentioned, the relevant child (children) makes the appropriate sound. Obviously the more often the animals are mentioned the more the children will love it; and they will join in with extra enthusiasm if all the animals have to 'speak' simultaneously now and again.

Dead Lions

Any time you want to give yourself and your helpers a break, try this game. All ages know it. All ages love it. All you have to do is call out the magic words, 'Now we're going to play Dead Lions.' You will be surprised at the delighted reaction you'll receive. They will immediately fall flat on the floor. If you're in a hall and the floor is dirty tell them to sit on chairs or stand up. Anybody who moves is eliminated. They are allowed to breathe and blink but if you catch them moving when they do so they are 'out'.

When they are caught out they will want to help you to catch the others. If you allow this they'll all be declared 'out' in a few seconds and your precious break will be over. The best time to play Dead Lions is just before refreshment time. When they are 'out' they can go to the toilet, wash their hands, come back and sit ready for their food.

Eliminate them a couple at a time. This prolongs the game and prevents an unruly mob jostling one another outside the toilet.

The Farmer's In His Den

A timeless old favourite. The children all hold hands in a circle. One child is chosen to stand in the middle of the circle. He is the farmer. The others walk round the farmer chanting: 'The farmer's in his den, the farmer's in his den, ee I, ee I, the farmer's in his den. The farmer wants a wife, the farmer wants a wife, ee I, ee I, the farmer wants a wife.'

The children in the circle stand still whilst the farmer chooses one of them to be his wife. She joins the farmer in the middle of the circle. The rest repeat their walkaround chanting: 'The wife wants a child, the wife wants a child, ee I, ee I, the wife wants a child.'

A child is selected by the wife and stands in the middle of the circle. The next chant is: 'The child wants a nurse.' It

38

follows the same pattern as before. Then they sing: 'The nurse wants a dog.' Finally: 'The dog wants a bone.' To end the game they all pat the dog *lightly* on the back, chanting: 'We all pat the dog, we all pat the dog, ee I, ee I, we all pat the dog.'

You ask the child representing the bone to remain in the circle as the farmer. The others join the circle and the game is repeated several times.

Tunnels

Three or four adult helpers stand in various parts of the room with legs astride. The youngsters line up and march along to some music. When they come to an adult (a tunnel) they crawl under her legs.

RP

Dusty Bluebells

An older or more extrovert child is chosen. Let's say her name is Emma. The others form a circle and hold hands. They raise their hands to form arches around the circle. Emma wanders at will in and out of the circle bobbing under the raised hands and arms. Everyone sings: 'In and out the dusty bluebells, in and out the dusty bluebells, in and out the dusty bluebells, who shall be my partner?'

At this point Emma stands behind someone in the circle. Let's say his name is Mark. She puts her hands on Mark's shoulders and pats them in turn. The children all sing: 'Pitter patter, pitter patter, on my shoulder, (three times) you shall be my partner.'

Emma again wanders in and out of the circle followed by Mark. The children either side of Mark in the circle link hands. At the end of the first chorus Emma puts her hands on another pair of shoulders and so on.

As the game progresses the line gets longer and longer and the circle smaller. End the game by asking the players to water the last two bluebells with their watering cans. Mime the action and say, 'Ssss, Ssss,' to simulate the water.

With a large number of children this game may drag a little. To prevent this, gradually speed up the singing and actions. If you detect they are becoming restless you can finish the game at any time — don't try to run it for its full term.

Ring-a-Ring-o-Roses

This oldie is ideal for toddlers. They form a circle, holding hands. One or more adults in the circle can be a great help directing the play. They walk around chanting: 'Ring a ring o roses, a pocket full of poses, atishoo, atishoo, we all fall down.'

On the word *down* they all squat on the floor. Repeat until they tire of it.

Here We Go Round The Mulberry Bush

The players hold hands and walk around a chair. They sing: 'Here we go round the mulberry bush, the mulberry bush, the mulberry bush. Here we go round the mulberry bush, on a cold and frosty morning.'

Then they let go hands, stand still and mime an action to the next lines: 'This is the way we clean our teeth, clean our teeth, clean our teeth. This is the way we clean our teeth, on a cold and frosty morning.' Holding hands again they sing the chorus and then change the mime. Other mimes are: comb our hair, brush our shoes, iron our clothes, saw up wood, walk along.

Hedgehogs

Have you got an old sheet or piece of material? It's all you need for this intriguing game. Ask the youngsters to stand around the room. Show them the cloth (it should be large enough to cover a child when crouching down), then say: 'This is a game of Hide and Seek. I'm going to cover someone with this cloth. The rest of you have to guess who is hidden without touching the cloth. All close your eyes.' See that they do this and say: 'Put your hands over your eyes so that you can't see. Turn round three times. One . . . two . . . three. Now crouch down on the floor and curl up like a tiny hedgehog.' Make sure no one is peeping as you cover one of them with the cloth. 'Now you can all stand up except the little hedgehog under the cloth. Can you guess who it is? Look around and see who is missing.'

Sometimes they guess quickly. If no guesses are forthcoming prompt them: 'Is it a boy or a girl hedgehog? I'll give you a clue . . . it's a girl . . . I think she has a red dress . . . her name begins with S . . .'

They will happily play this game over and over again. Many will be keen to be chosen as the hedgehog and may overwhelm you with requests to 'choose me'. Tell them you only select the best one who curls up quietly.

Rabbits

This game gives very young children a good opportunity to work off some energy and have lots of fun, without too much chaos.

All the children pretend to be rabbits, and bunny hop about the floor. Suddenly the adult in charge calls out, 'Danger!' Immediately all the rabbits must stop prefectly still until they hear the call, 'Danger over', when they start to hop again. Any rabbit who wobbles while there is danger is out of the game.

Rather than have a group of bored and miserable toddlers who are already 'out', you can use this game to extract children, in pairs perhaps, to go to the bathroom or find their places for tea.

Grandma's Footsteps

This is an old favourite, but still a winner. One child is Grandma, and stands at one end of the room facing the wall. The other children start at the far end of the room and creep silently towards Grandma. As soon as she hears a sound, Grandma turns round and sends anyone she sees moving back to the start. When another child succeeds in touching Grandma, they change places.

Frog Chase

This simple game is tag with a difference. Everyone has to crouch down and hop around like a frog. If the person chasing can't catch anyone, choose someone else. Anyone tagged becomes the new chaser.

One, Two, Buckle My Shoe

You need a large plastic sack for this game. A dustbin liner is ideal. Alternatively, use an old pillowcase.

Ask the children to each remove a shoe. Holding the sack open, ask them to pop their shoes in it. Mix them up and ask them to hold hands in a circle around you. When they are in position tell them to let go hands and sit down.

Tip all the shoes in a heap in the centre of the circle and retreat to a safe distance. When you say, 'One, two, three — GO!' they have to find their shoe and put it on. The first one to reach you is the winner.

Butterfly Net

This game can be played in a hall, or outdoors if you have a reasonable-sized garden. If you have a lawn, use this as the playing area.

Four children represent a butterfly net. They hold hands in a line. All the other players are butterflies. They flit around the area waving their hands up and down.

The 'net' children chase the butterflies and try to catch one by surrounding him. He then becomes part of the net by holding hands with the others. Then try to catch the other butterflies in a similar manner.

When only four are left they become the new net.

43

RP

The Robber

This 'sitting down' game involves every youngster in performing various actions and noises. You act as storyteller.

'I'm going to tell you the tale of Naughty Ned the robber. I'd like you all to join in. Can you make the noise of a police car?' Get them to do this.

'Now let's pretend to ride a bike. Hold the handlebars. Move your feet on the pedals. Ring the bell.' Again, see that they perform the actions correctly.

'Next, pretend to drive a car. Change gear — unless your car is automatic. Then we pretend to be a train.' Hold your hands beside you, thumbs uppermost, palms facing one another. Move them in circles. When the children have copied your actions say, 'Make the noise of a train whistle: Whooo ooo.'

'Now lets pretend we are jumbo jets. Hold your arms outstretched.' When they do this you'll find they all have a different 'noise' to accompany the action.

'Next, we pretend to be cowboys. They have a warcry. Would you all shout "Yahoo!". Then make a gun noise and pretend to fire pistols or rifles.'

'The last one is to pretend we are Indians. They have a warcry.' Pat your mouth quickly as you say 'Ooooh'.

'When they fire their arrows we all say, "Zing" and mime the action. Good. Now we're ready for the story.'

You tell the following tale repeating all the mimes and noises.

'Naughty Ned robbed a bank. He escaped on his bike . . . someone called the police who chased Ned in their car . . . Ned left his bike and jumped in his getaway car . . . the police were catching up . . . Ned arrived at the station and dashed on a train . . . He got off at the airport and boarded a jumbo jet . . . he landed in America. Amongst the cowboys and Indians. Cowboys — give your warcry . . . fire your guns . . . Indians — give your warcry . . . fire your arrows . . .'

'Naughty Ned was scared and gave himself up. He was flown back to England on another jet . . . then on a train . . . the police took him to jail in their car . . .'

'Ned promised not to rob any more banks.' To wrap up the 'game' you could ask the children to give themselves a round of applause for performing so well. If your memory isn't reliable, jot down the main actions on a card to remind you.

Party Plan For Tinies

11.00 a.m. Guests arrive and play with host's (chosen) toys.
11.45 a.m. Start with a very familiar game to get everyone relaxed (e.g. Ring-o-Roses, Farmer's in his Den). Alternate noisy and quiet games, ending with a restful one (e.g. Dead Lions).
12.15 p.m. Take all guests to the bathroom, a small group at a time, while the rest play another quiet game.
12.30 p.m. Lunch
1.00 p.m. Restart with a quiet game, or your own conjuring show.
1.20 p.m. Some more energetic games to end with.
1.30 p.m. Parents arrive to collect their children.

Checklist: A Tinies' Party

☐ Send invitations to your guests

☐ Buy gift, wrapping paper and card

☐ Wrap gift

☐ Go over the menu — the simpler the better for this age group

☐ Prepare snacks

☐ Bake birthday cake

☐ Check all the decorations and props you will be
needing

☐ Check the music

☐ Check that you have plenty of small prizes

☐ List the games in the order you will play them —
with spares listed in 'quiet' and 'energetic' columns

_____

_____

_____

_____

_____

_____

☐ List the telephone numbers of all of your little guests
under their first names. This will be invaluable if
any of them really collapses.

_____

_____

_____

_____

_____

Games For 5–8 Year Olds

Children in this age group can get very excited and noisy. However, the first six games listed below are guaranteed to calm them down and be good fun too.

Pass The Parcel

You are probably familiar with this game where the players sit in a circle and pass a parcel from one to the other as music plays. When the music stops the child holding the parcel undoes it, hoping to find a prize. This old favourite can flop dismally if you make the parcel in time-honoured fashion — one prize wrapped up in reams of paper. Your party guests will soon lose interest waiting for the finale. Try it this way. Use several small prizes. Wrap a prize in a piece of paper and Sellotape the paper. Wrap it in another piece of paper and Sellotape that. Then add *another* prize, wrap the next piece of paper and so on. Tell the children there are several prizes in your parcel — so be careful when you unwrap the paper — a prize may be there. This not only maintains interest but helps prevent a paper-throwing war.

Naughty Boy

One player is the teacher, the others are the pupils. The pupils sit in a row, the teacher faces them. The pupils pass a sweet from one to the other behind their backs. When the teacher calls out, 'Hands up naughty boy!' they all bring their closed hands from behind them and hold them in front of them. The teacher has three guesses to discover who has the sweet. If correct, she eats it and chooses someone else to be the teacher. If incorrect she joins the pupils and the person with the sweet becomes the new teacher.

Guess What

One child is chosen to hide outside the room. The others are shown a card with SWIM written on it. They are told to mime the word on the card in any way they wish. The youngster outside the room is recalled and has to guess what the children are miming. He has three guesses. If correct he wins a prize. Someone else is then selected to hide outside and another mime is performed. Here are some ideas for the mimes:
Ride a horse, have a bath, saw wood, play tennis, phone, eat

lunch, blow up a balloon, lick a lollypop. Write the mimes with a large felt tip on stiff paper or card.

Squirrels

A walnut is all you require for this game. A small rubber ball will do if you have difficulty supplying the nut. Sit the children in a circle and select one to stand in the middle of them. The ones in the circle are squirrels. They recite the following rhyme: 'Squirrel squirrel, tut tut tut, you have been into my hut. Squirrel squirrel, tut tut tut, which of you has got my nut?' As they say the rhyme they pass the nut from one to the other behind their backs. The child in the centre of the circle has her eyes closed and her hands over them. When the rhyme is finished the person who has the nut keeps it hidden behind them. The one in the circle has three guesses to detect who has the nut. If correct they win a prize and someone else has a go. With a small number of players, one guess is all they have. With a very large number, after each guess they receive a clue to how near they were. Give the clue by saying 'cold' or 'freezing' when they are way off the mark, and 'warm', 'hot' or 'boiling' when they are near.

They will all want a go but it may drag a little if you let them. When they are tiring tell them there will be another game later where they can win a prize.

Where's The Key?

Thread a key on to a long piece of string and tie the ends of the string to form a loop. The players sit in a circle holding the string with both hands. One of them has the key in her hand. Someone is chosen to sit in the centre of the circle with his eyes closed. The others pass the key around the string for a few seconds. Then the centre player opens his eyes and has to guess who is holding the key. When he isn't looking the players pass the key around secretly. If the key isn't discovered within two minutes someone else has a try. If the key is found the player in the centre gets a prize.

The Minister's Cat

This is an amusing game which offers plenty of scope for the inventive! It needs no props, and is an excellent standby whenever the children must of necessity be seated — such as in a car on the way to your party venue, or round the tea table.

The players say in turn, 'The minister's cat is a ---- cat', filling in the space with a word beginning with A. When each child has found an A word, you go round again, this time with words beginning with B.

Musical Arches

Two pairs of children hold hands like an arch above their heads. They stand one pair at each end of the room. The others line up and walk around the room and under the arches as the music plays. The arches bring their hands and arms down over each head as the players go underneath. When the music stops any children who are caught under an arch form a new arch. The last one to be caught wins. If there is a large number of children, ask the players to hold hands in pairs as they go round the room. In that case two will be caught under a single arch.

Musical Animals

Children love to play let's pretend. This simple game allows them to do this and win prizes. They dance or jump around as you play some lively music. When the music stops, tell them you will give a prize to the one who is best at pretending to be a cat. They meow, walk on all fours and act like cats. Select a suitable winner and tell her she will receive her prize at the end of the party. Ask the children to continue dancing and after about ten seconds stop the music once more. This time the winner will be the one who best imitates a dog. Other animals that allow children to give rein to their imaginations are: a lion, lamb, donkey, monkey, kangaroo, cow, pig, snake, chicken, bee.

This game allows you to give a prize to youngsters who are not very good at competing. It can be played by a wide age range — useful in joint parties where you have a mixture of tinies and older children.

Musical Bumps

Another game that sparks off an immediate interest in children. But the original version has two snags for today's child. In that version the players jig up and down to some music. When it stops they sit down as fast as they can. The last one to hit the floor each time is 'out' eventually leaving one winner.

The first snag is that those eliminated at the beginning of the game become bored. The second snag appears if you have a large number of children. Those left in the game towards the end are exhausted.

The answer is to reverse the rules. Nobody is eliminated. The *first* one to sit down each time the music stops wins a prize. You can finish the game when you think they've had enough. You may find that some try to anticipate when the music is going to stop and sit down whilst it is still playing. Tell them it doesn't count if they do that.

Musical Statues

This game has been updated. In the original version they all dance around to the music. When it stops they have to keep perfectly still. Anyone who moves is eliminated. The last one to be eliminated wins.

In this version nobody is 'out'. They pretend to play musical instruments as the music plays. When it stops they stand still and you give a prize to the best one each time. The following instruments give interesting mimes: piano, drums, violin, flute, trombone, trumpet, double bass, bag-pipes.

Ascot Hats

The props for this game are simple to make. Cut out circles, squares and any other shapes you like from magazines or newspapers. Pages from the Radio or TV Times are ideal for size. Give one of the shapes to each child. You explain, 'We are going to pretend we are at the Ascot races. Everyone wears hats there and they parade around to let everyone see what a nice hat they have. The sheets of paper are your hats. Put them on your heads. Sometimes at Ascot the wind blows and people lose their hats. In this game you all walk around slowly when the music plays. You mustn't touch your hat unless it comes off. Then you can put it back on again.'

Do this for a minute or two, then stop the music and explain a variation in the rules. 'We're going to do some-thing more difficult now. This time when the music stops you have to crouch down slowly. Again, you mustn't touch your hats unless they fall off.' Repeat the exercise for another minute or so. 'Now we've had a practise we'll do it again but when the music stops you have to sit down as fast as you can. No hands unless the hat flies off. I'll give a prize for the one who does it best each time.'

The Moonmen Race

This is a race with a difference. The competitors crouch

down. Their hands must be off the floor. They must race on their feet not their knees. Tell them they are moonmen who are very small. An amusing alternative when you have a large number of competitors is to divide them into a number of teams. Each team crouch down, one person behind the other. The ones behind the leaders put their hands on the shoulders of the child in front of them. The lines of mini-men waddling along always produces laughter.

Creepy Crawlies

One player faces a wall at one end of the room, which needs to be quite a big one. The others start at the other end and creep towards the solitary player. He can turn round when he likes. If he spots anyone moving they are sent back to the starting point. The first one to reach the wall player wins and takes his place. Repeat until they've had enough.

Commandos

Suitable for both sexes — in spite of its title — this game requires a few simple props. They are three chairs, and a broom or walking-stick. Near one end of the room put two chairs about a metre apart, backs toward one another. The broom is placed across the top rails of the chairs. The third chair is positioned near the opposite end of the room. The children line up behind the birthday child — he is the leader of the commandos. They have to follow their leader under the broom, back round the single chair and under the broom again. They must try not to dislodge the broom by moving it accidentally. Play some music as they follow one another. When they've gone round two or three times, stop

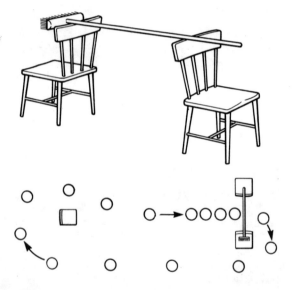

the music and lower the broom to the next level, the chair seats, and repeat the exercise. It doesn't matter if anyone moves the broom — they're still in the game. The winner is the one who performs the manoeuvres best — who moves the broom the fewest times. The lowest position is on the chair rungs. Re-align the chairs for this.

They seem to enjoy this game so much that you may find they'll want to play it again. If you're in a hall the floor could be dirty. In that case an old blanket or cloth should be placed on the floor under the two chairs with the broom.

Busy Bees

Ask the children to choose a partner. If there is an odd one out they are the queen bee. If not, you are the queen bee. The queen bee calls out various actions which the other children have to do. When they hear the command, 'Busy Bees' they all change partners — including the queen bee. There will be another child left without a partner and she becomes the new queen bee.

Examples of actions are: jump up and down, stand back to back, hold hands and skip, run around, walk about fast, hop around, sit on your partner's knee, hold hands and swing around.

If you write a list of the actions it can be given to each queen bee as a memory aid.

Traffic Jam

All the players stand at one end of the room. They represent cars. One player is a traffic policeman. He is at the opposite end of the room. When he calls out, 'Green' everyone jumps towards the policeman, pretending to drive a car. When they hear the command, 'Amber' they crouch down and walk. On the command, 'Red' they must keep perfectly still, in the crouched position.

Anyone who doesn't perform a command correctly goes back to the starting point. Any player who moves — even slightly — on the command 'Red' also goes back to the start. The first car to reach the policeman changes places with him. The policeman joins the cars and they all start from the other end of the room again.

Fishing

Cut out a number of small paper fish. The easiest way to do this is to cut a card template first and trace round it on to the paper. Hide the fish around the party room before the guests arrive. On the word 'go' the players have to find as many fish as they can in 5 minutes or so. Don't hide them too high up — the children may hurt themselves or damage ornaments trying to clamber after the fish.

Shunting Trains

Divide the children into two or more teams. They stand in line, one behind the other. They are goods trucks; their leaders are engines. If there is an odd child out he is the stationmaster. When the stationmaster waves his flag (a handkerchief) the engines *walk* forward to the opposite end of the room. Then they walk backwards to the next member of their team. The truck puts her hands on the engine's shoulders and they both walk to the opposite wall and back again. After each journey another truck links to the train. The first team to complete the journey linked together wins. You will need a big room, hall or garden to play this game successfully.

Postman

Before the party, write a list of countries or towns, so that there are enough to give one name to each child. Sit the children in a circle, with one blindfolded in the middle. Then call out that you are going to post something from one place to another. The two children representing those places must swap seats without being caught by the child in the middle.

If the organiser sends a postcard, the two children have to crawl across the circle. For a letter, they hop; for a telegram, they run; for a parcel, they skip.

Any child who moves when his 'place' has not been called, or who crosses the circle in the wrong manner, or who is caught by the one in the middle, loses a life. The winner, when you decide that everyone has had enough, is the child who has lost the fewest lives.

The Circus

One player is the ring-master, and stands blindfolded in the middle of a ring of the remaining children. They skip round until the ring-master shouts 'Stop!' He then points to one of the children and says, 'Make the noise of a -----', naming whatever circus animal he chooses. The child who is pointed to makes the noise, and the ring-master must guess who it is. If he succeeds, and he can ask for the noise to be repeated up to three times, the two children swap places. If he fails, he continues as ring-master.

Simon Says

This game is very simple, but always fun. One player is Simon, and stands facing the others. He then gives them orders to do whatever he does, such as hopping, putting his hands on his head, scratching his left ear and so on. 'Simon' does every action, but the others must only imitate him if he says, 'Simon says. . . .' If he gives an order without the words 'Simon says', the other children must remain stock still. Any child who moves when he should not have done is out, and can help judge the others. The last one in becomes Simon.

Squeak Piggy Squeak

All the players sit round in a circle, except one, who is blindfolded and holds a cushion. He walks round the inside of the circle, places the cushion in whatever lap he can find, and says, 'Squeak, Piggy, squeak' or, if you prefer, 'Grunt,

Piggy, grunt'. The player on whom he is sitting the squeaks (or grunts) three times, and the blindfolded child has to guess who is making the noise. If he guesses correctly, he and the child who squeaked (grunted) swap places. If he fails, he must try again.

Jump The Rope

This game can get quite energetic, and certainly needs the space provided by a garden or large hall. But it is always popular.

You will need three or four yards of rope or thick string, with a small weight tied securely on one end. A wooden cotton reel suits the purpose well. An adult stands in the middle of a big circle of the children, and swings the rope around, about an inch above the ground. To stay in the game the players must jump over the rope as it comes round. As more children drop out, the rope can be swung higher off the ground in order to make it more difficult to jump over.

Murder

In spite of its name, this is in fact quite a gentle game, and a useful one to reserve to the end of the party since it will not matter if some of the players are collected during its progress.

All the children sit in a circle on the floor, except one, who sits in the middle and is the detective. The detective must close his eyes while an adult goes round the circle and taps every child on the shoulder, except one, who is the murderer. The detective is then told to open his eyes. The aim is for the detective to spot the murderer, who 'kills' players one by one, by catching their eye and winking. As the players are murdered, they must fall over backwards and lie dead on the floor. When the murderer is discovered it is time to choose a new pair to play the leading roles; everyone will be keen to have a turn!

Wicked Witch

Place a sheet of newspaper in the centre of the room. Choose someone to be a wicked witch. They crouch down on the paper.

The other players walk around the witch chanting, 'We're not scared of the silly old witch.' Slowly the witch rises until she is standing up. When she reaches her full height she yells, 'I'm coming to get you!' and chases the others.

She touches one and tells them they are a statue. That child stands perfectly still. The next one tagged is turned into a worm and wriggles their body around. Another is told to be a helicopter and spins round with arms outstretched.

The fourth child tagged becomes the wicked witch and crouches on the newspaper. The tagged players join the rest in walking round the new witch and the game is repeated.

The witch can vary the mime whenever she tags someone. To add to the suspense she should rise and sink back a couple of times before reaching her full height.

A Wink Or A Nod

Divide the children into two equal groups. Make a large circle of chairs — one for each girl plus an extra one. Ask the girls to sit on the chairs. A boy stands behind each chair including the empty one. An odd one out acts as referee.

The lad behind the empty chair looks around at the girls. At a suitable moment he winks or nods at one girl. She has to dash from her chair to the empty one. The boy standing behind her tries to stop her by placing both of his hands on her shoulders.

If he succeeds, she remains where she is and the boy who winked tries someone else. If the girl escapes she sits on the empty chair. The boy who failed to restrain her then acts as 'winker.'

Top Ten

Record small segments of ten pop tunes leaving a short silent gap between numbers. Make a list of titles and artists.

Give each guest paper and pencil. Play each piece of music allowing 30 seconds or so for the children to write the tune title and artist.

Score points for each tune and artist named correctly.

Dick Turpin

This is a story-time game where the children sit down and join in various actions. You are the storyteller. You could select suitable 'actors' to play the principal parts if you wish.

When choosing 'helpers' say you'll select the best ones sitting nicely and quietly. This avoids a mad rush as everyone tries to get in on the act.

Choose an older boy and girl to play Dick Turpin and his wife. Let's assume their names are Mark and Emma. Ask one to stand on your left and the other one on your right.

'This is the story of Dick Turpin,' you begin. 'Hands up anyone who knows what he was?' If nobody knows, you say, 'He was a highwayman. He rode a horse called Black Bess. He had two guns and held up stagecoaches.'

Tell them that Mark is Dick Turpin and Emma his wife. 'When I say *Dick Turpin rode across the fields*,' you explain, 'I'd like you all to pat your chests.' You demonstrate by patting your chest to the rhythm of horse's hoofs. Ask the children to copy you.

'When I say *he went along the road* you pat your legs.' This time you do the same rhythm on your thighs.

'If I say *the cows mooed*, you all moo like a cow,' you continue, rehearsing them in the sound.

'When I say *the ducks quacked* you quack like a duck.' Pause as they do this.

'When I say *the pigs grunted* you make the noise of a pig.' This produces some amusement as they snort in various ways.

'Now we're ready for the story,' you tell them. At each stage you lead them in the actions and noises.

'Dick Turpin decided to rob a farm instead of a stage-coach. He mounted his horse. What was her name? Black Bess. They went along the road . . . across the fields . . . arrived at the farm. The cows mooed . . . the ducks quacked . . . the pigs grunted . . . Dick knocked on the door. When the farmer opened it Dick said, "Hands up! your money or your life!"' (Ask Mark to say the line, holding his fingers like two guns.)

'The farmer gave him 10p. Dick mounted his horse. What was her name? Black Bess. They rode across the fields . . . along the road . . . Back at the farm the cows mooed . . . (etc).

'Dick arrived home and showed his wife the 10p. She said, "That's not enough for the supermarket"' (ask Emma to repeat the words). And she hit Dick on the head with a sausage. (Emma mimes this. Alternatively, give her a balloon to serve as a sausage).

'Dick mounted his horse again. What was her name? Black Bess. He went along the road . . . (etc).

'This time the farmer gave him 50p. He mounted his horse once more (etc).

'His wife was pleased this time. She gave him a big kiss and they all lived happily ever after.'

The kiss produces amused reaction from everyone as Mark will probably recoil from Emma's advances.

Although this seems a lot to learn, most is repetition. If you're uncertain, write a cue on a postcard. This game is ideal to insert between more lively ones and maintains the interest of every child.

What's The Time Mr Wolf?

One child is chosen to be Mr Wolf. He walks around followed by the others. They all chant, 'What's the time Mr Wolf?' repeatedly. The wolf calls out various times. Nothing happens until he says, 'One o'clock — lunch time!' When this happens everybody has to run to safety — usually by touching a wall. Anyone who is touched by the wolf becomes the new wolf — the old one joining the others.

Charge Of The Light Brigade

This game is ideal for outdoors or in a hall. All the players except one are at one end of the area. One child is in the middle of the area. On the command, 'Charge!' all the players gallop from one end of the area to the other trying to avoid the player in the middle. He has to try to touch the others. Any who are tagged join the middle player and the game proceeds in the same way. The last one to be tagged wins.

Three Blind Mice

One child is selected to be a farmer's wife. The others hold hands in a circle around her. They walk around singing:

'Three blind mice, three blind mice,
See how they run, see how they run,
They all ran after the farmer's wife,
Who cut off their tails with a carving knife,
Did you ever see such a thing in your life?
As three blind MICE!'

The last word is emphasised. As soon as they sing it the farmer's wife chases them. They dash for the sides of the room. If one is tagged they become the farmer's wife. If not, the existing wife has two more tries. If still unsuccessful you select another child to be the wife.

Kangaroo Race

For this game you want six pieces of card and a dice. Each card has a number on it — from 1 to 6. The cards should be fairly large — approximately 7 ins x 5 ins (178 mm x 127 mm).

Six children are each given a numbered card and line up at one end of the room. The others take it in turn to throw the dice. The player with the card corresponding to the number on the dice takes one jump forward. Both feet must be together before they jump. They stand on the spot where they land. The first one to reach a finishing line wins the race. Another six are chosen for the next race and so on.

If you have a large number of children in a hall or out-doors you could have two sets of numbered cards. In that case whenever a number comes up on the dice two players jump towards the winning post. A couple of chairs could be placed to mark the winning line. Every child will want to have a go in this unusual race. At the end you may have only two or three children in the last race so select others who have already raced to make up the number.

Musical Laps

This game is best if you have equal numbers of boys and girls. It is similar to musical chairs but much more lively. Line up some chairs — one less than the number of boys in the game.

As you play some lively music the boys all walk round the chairs. The girls sit around the room. When the music stops each boy grabs a girl, takes her to a chair and sits down with the girl on his lap. The boy who fails to find a seat is out.

Remove another chair and repeat the play. When only two chairs are left spread them far apart. When only one is left, place it in the centre of the room. Ask two of the strongest lads to stand several metres either side of the chair.

The remaining two players have to go round the standing boys.

Partners

Divide the children into two equal groups. If there's an odd one out they can help you give the instructions.

Ask one group to hold hands in a circle. The other group hold hands in a circle around the first one.

You play some music. The inner circle walk or jig around in one direction. The outer group go in the opposite direction.

You stop the music and each outer player chooses one of the inner players as a partner. You read out an action that they have to do. Here are a few examples:

1 Give your partner a piggyback.

2 Hold hands and spin in a circle.

3 Tickle your partner until they laugh.

4 Hold your partner's ankles as they walk on their hands — like a wheelbarrow.

5 Sing your partner a nursery rhyme.

6 Pull a funny face until your partner laughs.

7 Hold hands with your partner and both of you hop on one leg.

8 Touch the tips of your noses together and walk round in a circle.

9 One of you crouch on all fours and the other one sit on their back — like riding a horse.

10 Kiss your partner and say, 'Thank you for being my partner.'

Place Your Bets

Choose six children to be racehorses. Each one holds a piece of card with a number on — one to six. You also need two dice.

Ask the other youngsters to line up along both sides of the room. One child on each side has a dice. Everyone chooses one of the 'horses' they'd like to win.

When the dice are thrown the numbers determine which horse moves towards the winning post (two chairs at the opposite end of the room.) They move by taking one step forward. A double (for example, two threes) means horse number three takes *two* strides.

The 'spectators' take it in turn to throw the dice. At the end of the race another six horses take their places. If there's time you could have a winner's race. If there are less than six for the last race make up the number with losers from other races.

If there is a large number of children at your party you could have twelve in each race and have two of each number. You still use only two dice though.

Clothes Show

Do you have some old clothing, hats, shoes etc? They can be used in this game. Some newspaper and sticky tape can also be used.

Divide your players into two — half are models and half are dressmakers. Give the dressmakers two or three sheets of paper each and some of the clothing. They are allowed ten minutes or so to dress their models. You help with the sticky tape by cutting off lengths as required. The best dressed model wins a prize for herself and her partner.

Animal Choir

Arm yourself with a ruler and you are ready for this noisy game. You are the conductor of your choir — the children.

Ask each one to pretend to be a certain animal. They must be animals that make a particular noise — dog, cat, lion, donkey, cow, pig, snake, mouse, chicken, lamb.

You'll probably have more children than suitable animals so you can have several dogs, cats etc.

You lead them in an animal rendition of 'Happy Birthday' or any other tune you think suitable. They make their animal noise in tune with the music.

Groups

This game is suitable for older children with fairly good imaginations. Divide them into small groups of four or more. One person from each group is chosen to leave the room.

While outside they think of something ridiculous or difficult to guess. You could have a list to give them some ideas.

The ones outside the room re-enter and join a *different* group. The group members have to guess the object or idea thought of. They must ask questions that need a 'yes' or 'no' answer.

As soon as someone in a group guesses the object all the children who were outside the room join that group. They now have a better chance to guess the next object.

Each group sends out another representative and a different object is selected. Continue until one group has absorbed all the players.

Here are a few ideas to get you started:

1 The Prime Minister's toenails.
2 Sunset in the Sahara Desert.
3 Father Christmas's whiskers.
4 An Easter egg.
5 A chimney pot.
6 London Symphony Orchestra.
7 Jack and the Beanstalk.
8 Liquorice Allsorts.
9 Halloween.
10 Charlie's Aunt.

The groups should ask questions like: Is it an animal? Is it a mineral? Is it a vegetable? Is it human? Is it in this country? Can you eat it?

Guessing Game

Beforehand, write a list of objects and a question related to them. The objects must be on a table so your party guests can see them. Each person has pencil and paper to write their guesses on. The one with most correct wins a prize. Here are a few ideas:

1 A magazine page. Guess how many words on it.
2 A cup of rice. How many grains are in it?
3 A ball of wool. How long is it when unravelled?
4 A box of pins. How many are in it?
5 A jar of peas or sweets. How many does it hold?
6 The birthday cake. How much does it weigh?
7 A jug of water. How much water is in it?

Tell the players that they do not have to guess the exact number, which would be almost impossible. The nearest correct guess wins each time.

Shepherds

One party guest is chosen to be a shepherd. Another is his dog. They are both at one end of the room. The dog is blindfolded and on all fours. The rest of the children are obstacles.

The obstacles stand or sit around the room. They position themselves after the dog has been blindfolded.

The shepherd has to guide his dog verbally through the obstacles to the opposite side of the room. He uses commands like, 'Take two steps forward, three to the left, turn slightly to the right,' etc.

Once a command is given it cannot be altered until the dog has carried it out. The only exception is if the dog could hurt himself.

The shepherd must stay put — he isn't allowed to walk behind his dog.

At larger parties in a hall or outdoors you can have two or three shepherds and their dogs. This adds to the fun because a dog may obey the commands of the wrong shepherd.

Winners are decided on a time basis. The pair who complete the course in the shortest time win.

Fox And Chickens

You need a large area for this game. One child is asked to be a cockerel. They stand at one corner of the area. A second youngster is a fox and stands in the centre of the area. The other players are chickens and stand at the end of the area opposite the cockerel.

The cock crows and calls one of the chickens by name. If they are strangers he describes the chicken's appearance — 'The chicken in the red dress and blonde hair . . .'

The chicken named has to join the cock without being tagged by the fox. If tagged, the chicken stands or sits on that spot. This provides cover for succeeding chickens.

When they have all run the gauntlet you choose someone else to be the fox and cockerel.

Cuckoo's Nest

This game is suitable for larger groups. Divide the guests into groups of three or four — let's say three. Two children in each group hold hands. They represent birds' nests. A third player stands in each nest — they are birds.

You need two or three children who are not part of a nest group. They walk or run around flapping their arms like wings.

When you call out 'Cuckoo!' all the nested birds must find a new home. The homeless ones try to find a nest during the changeover.

Pat-A-Balloon

This can be played anywhere. All you require is a round balloon. Form the children into two equal teams. They sit on the floor in straight lines, facing one another about a metre apart.

Each team has to try to tap the balloon over the heads of their opponents so it falls to the floor behind them. You decide the first team to 'kick off' by tossing a coin.

You must referee the game strictly. The rules are simple.

1   Players must always be seated.

2   The balloon must be tapped not punched.

If anyone breaks a rule the opposing team is given the balloon. Alternatively, the offending player is removed from the game for two minutes.

Half time is called after 5 minutes. The team who lost the toss have the balloon for the second half kick-off.

The Wizard Of Woz

One player is blindfolded and given a ruler to hold. He stands still whilst the others walk around him in a circle. They all chant, 'We're going to see the Wizard of Woz,' over and over again.

When they have done this a few times the wizard shouts 'STOP'. He points his ruler (his magic wand) towards someone in the circle. That person holds the other end of the ruler. The wizard asks three questions. His victim answers in a disguised voice. They can speak in a high pitch, holding their nose etc.

The wizard then has to guess who the person is. (He can't ask the question: 'What is your name?' of course!)

Sample questions are: 'What is your favourite meal?' 'How old are you?' 'Recite a rhyme.'

If the wizard guesses correctly he changes places with his victim, who dons the blindfold and holds the ruler. If he fails he is allowed two more tries. Still unsuccessful? You choose another child to be the wizard.

Washday

You need a piece of clothesline or thick string, six pegs and six handkerchiefs or squares of rag. Two youngsters hold the clothesline between them. It should be taut and at a height the others can easily reach.

Divide the other children into two equal teams. They line up on opposite sides of the clothesline and as far away from it as possible. Each team leader has three pegs and handkerchiefs.

When you give the signal to start they both rush to the line and peg their 'washing' to the line. Then they dash back to their teams and touch the next team member.

These two run to the line and unpeg the washing. Then rush back to their teams to hand the pegs and washing to the next competitor in line. And so on. The first team to all finish one of the operations wins.

You must referee firmly to see that the handkerchiefs are properly pegged. And that team members don't edge towards the line. It would be wise to have some spare pegs in case one breaks.

Balloon Race

All you require for this game is plenty of room, some balloons (round) and drinking straws. You need a balloon and straw for every child in the race. Six at a time should be ideal.

Place two chairs at one end of the room to mark the finishing line. Competitors blow their balloons along the course. Winners of each race have a play-off to decide the ultimate winner.

Human Alphabet

Another game for large numbers of guests. Split them into groups of six or more. You play some music and they dance or jump around. When you stop the music you call out a letter.

They have to form that letter by moving into its shape (viewed from above). They can hold hands if necessary. When they've done so they crouch down. You select the best shape to win the round. It isn't essential that *every* person in a group forms part of any letter.

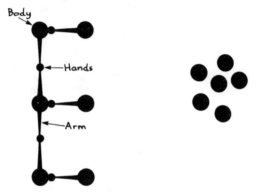

Musical Dash

Ideal for a hall. Divide the players into teams. A small number form two teams facing one another in lines. A larger number can be formed into three or four teams positioned as three or four sides of a square.

Place a newspaper on the floor in the centre of the room. On this you place matchboxes — one for each team.

As the music plays one child from the end of each team rushes to the newspaper, grabs a matchbox and takes it to the second team member. That person runs back and deposits the matchbox on the newspaper. And so on.

Whenever the music stops any player holding a matchbox has to give it to the previous member of their team.

If the teams have even numbers the last member to place the box on the paper wins for that team.

If they have odd numbers the last member to get back to their place with a matchbox wins for their team.

Hokey Cokey

This old adult party dance has become increasingly popular with today's children. A useful tip is to have two or three adults who know the routine amongst the children. Any child who is uncertain can then copy an adult.

You can buy a tape of the music but it may not be at a suitable tempo for your guests. Here's the routine:

They all form a circle. Singing the following words they perform actions to suit the words.

'Put your left hand in, your left hand out,
In, out, in, out and shake it all about,
You do the Hokey Cokey (wave hands to and fro
    sideways),
And you turn around,
That's what it's all about.
Oh Hokey, Cokey, Cokey (Walk forward four steps and
    back again,
then repeat two more times)
Knees bend, arms stretch, rah, rah, rah.' (Clap hands for
    the rahs.)

The above sequence is repeated with right hand, left leg, right leg, left side, right side. The final part — whole self — is performed at a fast pace, jumping forward and back again several times. Also the guests all hold hands as they jump.

Party Plan For 5–8 Year Olds

3.00 p.m. Guests arrive and play Hunt the Thimble.
3.15 p.m. Musical Animals, Creepy Crawlies, What's the Time Mr Wolf and other energetic games, alternated (not too often) with quieter ones such as Naughty Boy, Guess What etc.
4.00 p.m. Tea
4.30 p.m. Home conjuring show.
4.45 p.m. Musical Bumps, Pass the Parcel and other old favourites.
5.15 p.m. Announce last game, firmly, and make it a good noisy finale.
5.25 p.m. All guests collect a balloon and party bag/slice of cake.
5.30 p.m. Parents arrive to collect guests.

Checklist: Afternoon And Evening Parties

- Send invitations to your guests

- Buy gift, wrapping paper and card

- Wrap gift

- Go over the menu

- Prepare snacks

- Bake birthday cake
- Check all the decorations and props you will be needing

- Check the music

☐ Check prizes

☐ Move furniture and ornaments out of the play area

☐ List the games in the order they will be played —
prepare for more than you think you will need

_____

_____

_____

_____

_____

_____

☐ List the telephone numbers of your guests in the
event of an accident

_____

_____

_____

_____

_____

_____

☐ Drinks for parents collecting their children

Games for Older Folk

Older children will be bored and insulted by 'baby games.' However, the games given here are all popular, even with today's sophisticated youngsters, because they are intriguing or funny. The first 11 are quite quiet; the rest are definitely not! All could be played and enjoyed by seven or eight year olds, but will also be popular with any slightly older children who come to the party.

Chinese Chopsticks

A few simple props are used in this game. Two saucers, two knives, some Smarties, a dice and shaker. Prepare the dice by sticking some white paper on it to cover the spots. Mark some pseudo Chinese characters on the sides of the dice — one in red the others in black.

The players sit in a circle. One saucer is filled with Smarties and put on the floor in the middle of the circle. The empty saucer is beside it with the two knives on it. The children take it in turn to throw the dice. Explain that it is a Chinese dice, and so that they can recognise the number six you have marked it in red. When someone throws the red six they all shout out 'Chinese chopsticks'. The person who threw the six takes the knives and tries to transfer as many Smarties as she can to the empty saucer. She must transfer them one at a time. When she hears the next shout of 'Chinese chopsticks' she takes all the sweets she has transferred and the next one who threw six has a go.

Name The Advert

Cut out about 20 adverts from magazines or papers. Also cut out or obliterate the product names. Give the competitors paper and pencils. They have to write down as many of the products and brand names as they can. The one with the most correct wins. If you haven't many pencils saw them in half and sharpen the blunt ends.

Memory Man

Cut out pictures of different objects from magazines for example, a car, house, animal. You need 15 altogether. Give the players paper and pencils. They have two minutes to study the pictures. Remove the pictures and give them another five minutes to write down as many pictures as they can remember. The person with most correct wins.

Guess The Drawing

Divide the guests into two teams, each with a leader. The leaders have a pad and pencil each. You are at the opposite end of the room with a list of objects. You whisper the first object to the team leaders. They dash to their teams and draw the object as quickly and simply as they can. When someone in their team guesses the object another team member comes to you for the next one and so on. Those doing the drawing are not allowed to talk or convey information in any way other than drawing. The teams must whisper the answer in case their opponents overhear. Adult helpers should be at hand to see there is no cheating. Here is a list of suitable objects: pig, house, trombone, boat, phone, plane, hat, chair, giraffe, wheelbarrow, cigar, dustbin, television set, car, bird.

Follow My Leader

The children sit in a circle and one is sent out of the room. The others choose a leader. The leader starts an action, for example, combing her hair. The others copy their leader. The player outside enters and stands in the centre of the circle. He has to guess who the leader is. The leader must keep changing the action, waiting until the centre player is looking the other way of course. The centre player has two minutes to detect the leader. If he succeeds he becomes the new leader and the previous one leaves the room. If he fails he is told who the leader is and he chooses a new one. Other mimes the leader can do are: rub tummy, scratch ear, wink, wave, laugh.

Words

Another pencil and paper game. The players have six minutes to make as many words as they can from the word BIRTHDAY. Each word must have at least three letters and be in the dictionary. No proper names or foreign words allowed.

Disguises

Cut out several pictures of famous people. Draw moustaches, dark glasses or beards on them with felt tips. The guests have to guess who the pictures are. The one with most correct wins.

Touch And Guess

Several objects are put into an old pillow case. Sew up the open end. The players have pencils and paper and have to guess the objects by feeling them through the material. Allow them five minutes. The one with most correct guesses wins.

Ideas for objects are: a ball, cotton reel, matchbox, large button, brush, coin, comb, beads, peg, spoon, key, ring.

Listen Carefully

All the players have pencil and paper. They have to guess what actions are being performed by listening to their sound on a tape recorder. If you preface each noise with 'number one, number two,' and so on they can number their answers. The one with most correct wins.

Here are a few ideas for your recordings: strike a match, pour water, chink coins, screw up paper, pull a cork from a bottle, brush a coat, rattle some keys, tear paper, shuffle a pack of cards, start the car, burst a paper bag, sharpen a pencil.

A variation if you have a video is to record some famous people speaking or singing — comedians, actors, politicians. Play the video through the TV set minus the picture. When they've written down their guesses run through the video again with the picture appearing.

Video Detectives

This game can be played without a video camera but using video equipment enhances the effect. An apron or sheet, a hat and a handkerchief are your other props. Set the video camera well away from the TV set. The children sit in front of the TV with their eyes closed. You choose half a dozen children by tapping their shoulders. They all leave the room. One at a time they put on the disguise. The apron or sheet is tied around the neck to hide clothing which may give a clue. The handkerchief is put round the face and tied at the back. The hat is pulled well down.

When disguised the player parades in front of the video camera or directly in front of the audience, and the others have three guesses to discover who he is. An amusing addition is to ask the one in disguise to recite a rhyme holding their nose. You can give a prize to anyone who is first to discover the identity of the child in disguise. If they fail, the disguised one wins something.

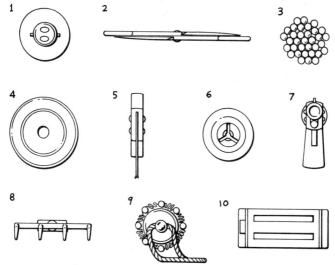

Guess What

Various objects are drawn or videoed from an unusual angle. The children have to guess the objects. The person with the most correct wins. If you are using a video camera try to get the objects as large as possible in the frame. The following will give you some ideas:

1 Light bulb viewed from the narrow end

2 Pair of scissors open and edge on

3 Bunch of matches end on

4 Rear view of a flower pot

5 Front view of a saw, from the blade end

6 Drill chuck, end on

7 Toy gun from barrel end

8 Garden fork from prong end

9 Closed umbrella from handle end

10 Toaster, top view

Human Spelling

You need eight large pieces of card. Draw the following letters on four of the cards — one letter for each card: S T O P. Draw the same letters on the other set of cards but in a different colour.

Two teams of four play the game. The others are judges. Each team has a set of letters. When you call out a word they have to line up to spell that word correctly. It must be able to be read by the judges not by the team. The words you call out are: STOP, POTS, POST, TOPS, SPOT. The first team to spell a word correctly score a point. The winners are the ones who score most points.

Choose different teams until they have all had a go, and then, if the children wish, play winners against winners in a knockout. Vary the order of calling out the words.

Pairs Chase

Two players hold hands and try to touch or tag a third person. When they succeed, that person also holds hands so three children are chasing the others. When a fourth is caught they split up into two pairs holding hands. Continue until all are tagged. The last two start the next session.

A variation of this game is for all those tagged to hold hands with the original two players. Eventually a long 'croco-dile' of children holding hands are snaking about trying to catch those left in the game.

Clearly a large hall or garden is essential for this game!

Nosey Parker

This is an unusual race. Competitors push table-tennis balls over a short distance using only their noses. Keep an eagle eye open for any cheating.

Squirrels And Nut

A small rubber ball to represent a nut is in the centre of the room. Two equal teams sit in rows opposite one another at the sides of the room. If there is an odd player left out she can act as caller, if not you do so. Each person in team A is designated by a number. The opponents in team B have the same numbers but start at the opposite end of their team.

The caller shouts out any number, say, 3. Number three from each team dashes to grab the 'nut' and then return to his place without being touched by his opponent. If he succeeds his team scores a point. If he fails the other side score one. The tag cannot be made until someone is holding the 'nut'. If two squirrels arrive at the same time they must watch for a suitable moment to snatch the 'nut'.

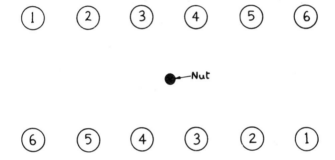

Stepping Stones Race

You need two pages from magazines for each player. They hold one and stand on the other. The idea is to use the papers as stepping stones to race from one end of the area to the other.

If outdoors the players place one page down in front of them, step on it, pick up the one behind them and so on. If in a hall it is possible to slide the papers along alternately with the feet.

Earth, Moon And Space

All the players kneel in a row. When you call, 'Earth' their hands must be on the floor. If you say, 'Moon' they must put their hands on their heads. On the command, 'Space' their hands should be in the air. Anyone who fails to perform the commands correctly is 'out'. When they are 'out' they can help you to judge. The last one to be 'out' wins.

Vary the pace of your commands and the volume of your voice. Another ploy to catch clever ones is to give the same command twice. Or try this: call the same two commands over and over and suddenly change to the third command. They will become conditioned to moving to the first two positions and falter when the third suddenly crops up.

Space Rockets

Buy some balloons. Sausage shaped ones are best but round ones will do so long as they are all the same size and shape. Mark them with consecutive numbers using a ball-point pen or waterproof felt-tip.

Line up the competitors and give each one a balloon. They blow up their balloons and hold the mouths to prevent the air escaping. When you say 'Ready — steady — go,' they all let their balloons go. The one that travels farthest wins.

Blow Me Down

All the players stand holding a sheet. A feather is placed in the centre. When someone calls out, 'Blow' they all try to blow the feather over the edge of the sheet on to another player. When this happens, that player is 'out'. When only two players are left, four of the others hold the corners of the sheet. It is surprising how much fun is generated by this game. I remember playing it at a 21st birthday party and winning by conserving my breath until the feather came my way!

Balloon Relay

Divide the guests into two or more teams. Odd ones left out can be judges to ensure there is no cheating. Each team leader has a balloon. On the command 'ready, steady, GO,' the balloons are passed over their heads to the back of the teams. The last team member runs to the front and continues passing the balloon back. The others shuffle back a little to make room. The first leader to return to the front of her team wins the race.

One variation is for the players to tap the balloons over their heads instead of passing directly to the next pair of hands. Others, which cause much amusement, are to pass a tangerine from one to another under the chin, or to pass a balloon gripped between the knees — no hands!

Peas Please

Place two chairs at one end of the room with an empty cup or beaker on each. At the opposite end of the room put two chairs with a cup of dried peas on each. Two teams stand around the chairs with the empty cups. Each player has a straw. If there is an odd one out, they can be referee. On the command, 'Ready, steady, go' the first players in each team run to the cups of peas and pick up a pea by sucking with the straws. Then they dash to the empty cups and drop the peas in them. The team members take turns and the first team to transfer all the peas wins. The number of peas must be the same as, or a multiple of the number in the team. If a pea drops the player is allowed to recover it, with the straw, from wherever it falls.

An alternative idea is to use two squares of tissue or newspaper instead of the cups and peas. In this case the leaders transfer the paper from one chair to the other (via the straws). The next team member takes the paper back to the first chair and so on.

To And Fro

You need two boxes of matches with the same number of matches in each box. The number is immaterial. Divide the children into two teams and line them up side by side. The child at the end of each line is the leader and holds a matchbox. On the command 'Go' each leader takes her matches out one at a time and gives them to the next member of the team. He passes them to the third person and so on down the line. The last player passes the matches back up the line but they go *behind* everybody. Thus some matches are going one way in front of their bodies and some are going the opposite way behind their backs. The leaders count the matches as they arrive back and when all are in their boxes they shout 'finished'. The first to do so wins. The game can be repeated a few times with a play-off at the end if necessary.

Tennis Ball Race

Seat the players on chairs, facing each other in two rows about a yard apart. The first player in each row is given a tennis ball, which they must balance on their feet. At the word 'Go', these two first players must pass their tennis balls on to the next player in their row, by wriggling their feet and ankles. Hands must not be used on any account. The aim is to get the ball to the other end of the row before the opposing team does. The fun lies in the contortions of the players as they struggle to pass the ball without dropping it — because whenever the ball is dropped it must go back to the start of the row!

Match Box Race

This is very similar to the Tennis Ball Race, but in this game the two teams must pass the outer case of a match box from one nose to the next!

Cat And Dog

One player is chosen to be the cat. The others are the dogs, and stand in a circle with their hands behind their backs, facing inwards. The cat walks round the outside of the circle. Whenever she wishes she taps the hand of one of the dogs giving a loud 'meow'. The dog chases after the cat, trying to touch her before she reaches his place in the circle and takes it. If he fails, he becomes the cat and taps another hand. If he succeeds he goes back to his place in the circle and the cat touches someone else. Usually this game requires a fair amount of room. If space is limited and there is a danger that over-enthusiastic players could knock into things tell them they must walk not run.

Party Plan For Older Folk

4.30 p.m. Guests arrive and join in a Treasure Hunt or game of Giant Noughts and Crosses.

4.45 p.m. Start with energetic games such as Nosey Parker, Squirrels and Nut. Alternate one quiet game to every two noisy ones, ending with a paper and pencil game before tea.

5.45 p.m. Tea.

6.15 p.m. Guess the Drawing and Video Detectives.

6.45 p.m. A couple of noisy games to finish off with, such as Peas Please or Blow Me Down.

7.00 p.m. Parents arrive to collect guests. Offer them a glass of wine or a soft drink as the game draws to a close.

Checklist: Parties For Older Folk

☐ Send invitations to your guests

☐ Buy gift, wrapping paper and card

☐ Wrap gift

☐ Go over menu

☐ Prepare snacks

☐ Bake birthday cake

☐ Check decorations and props

☐ Check music

☐ Check prizes

☐ Move furniture and ornaments out of the living area if necessary

☐ List the games in the order they are to be played

_____

_____

_____

_____

_____

_____

☐ List the telephone numbers of your guests in the event of an accident

_____

_____

_____

_____

_____

_____

_____

_____

_____

_____

☐ Prepare drinks for parents collecting their children

Pencil And Paper Games

As soon as children can read and write, a whole new world of games opens up. The ones that follow are popular at any time, and can be particularly useful if your young guests are in a restaurant where the more active amusements will not be appreciated. They can all be played either by individual children or in pairs if preferred.

Find The Word

Give each child or group a pencil and paper, and a long word such as EXTRAORDINARY. All the players have to do is write down as many words as they can using the letters in the long word. Give prizes for the most words and the longest word.

Guess The Smell

Fill about six bottles or jam jars with different smelly substances such as washing-up liquid, garlic, coffee, lavender. Wrap each container in paper so that the contents cannot be seen. Number the jars and pass them round the players who must smell the contents and write down what they think each substance is.

Guess The Objects

Put about twenty objects on a small tray such as a button, pin, feather, etc. Give each child a pencil and paper. When the players have studied the objects on the tray for a couple of minutes, remove it and ask them to write down as many of the objects as they can remember. Give a prize for the longest list.

Call My Bluff

This game is best played when you have only eight or so children, and can cause much hilarity.

Divide the children into two groups. The organiser chooses an obscure word from the dictionary and reads it out. All the members from one team write down an imaginary definition and hand their papers to the organiser, who reads them — and the real definition — out loud. The second team consult each other to decide which is the correct definition. If they are right they score a point; if they are wrong the first team score a point. The first team to score five points wins.

To speed the game up and prevent anyone from getting bored, you can give both teams their words at the same time, so that they can all be writing their definitions at once.

Questions And Answers

Everyone is given a slip of paper, on which to write a question. The papers are then folded over, collected, shuffled and redistributed. Each player then writes an answer, without of course looking at the original question. When everyone has finished, the papers are collected again, and each player picks one at random to read out loud. The results are generally amusing, but if, as it sometimes will, vulgarity begins to creep in, it is best to move on to another game before matters get out of hand!

Consequences

Each player is given a long slip of paper and a pencil. They are then told to write at the top of the paper an adjective suitable for a man, and to turn the paper down, after which they must pass it to their neighbour. The next player should add the name of a man and fold the paper on before passing it on. No one must look at what is written under the folds. This writing, turning down and passing on goes on until the following are on the papers: adjective suitable for a man, man's name, adjective suitable for a woman, woman's name, name of a place where the two could meet, what he said to her, what she said to him, what the consequence was and what the world said.

The papers are then collected, mixed up, and drawn by the players, who read each one out loud.

Conjuring

Why not present your own magic show? Better still, if you are preparing all the food and organising the games, ask another adult to present a few simple magic tricks. The ones described here are suitable for various age groups from six upwards. The 'mind reading' or 'prediction' tricks, for example, are suitable for older children.

Conjuring provides an interesting break from the games and gives you breathing space. A good time for such a performance is after they've had refreshments. It is better that they sit quietly for a while after they've eaten.

The tricks described here need few props and are not difficult to perform. Although they appear simple it is essential that the performer practises the tricks privately first. Children can be a critical audience and are not easily fooled.

If you are really keen why not make a conical wizard's hat? Decorate it with a few stars — it will lend an air of authenticity to the magician. A magic wand can be made from dowelling or a piece of paper rolled into a tube and glued. Approximate size: 12 in long (305 mm) by ½ in diameter (12 mm). It is usually coloured black with white ends — the white parts 1½ in (38 mm) long.

Royal Transposition

What the audience see:

The magician shows three cards — a jack, queen and king. They are placed in a box. The queen and king are removed and put in the magic man's pocket. The queen changes places with the jack.

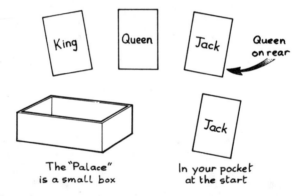

The "Palace" is a small box

In your pocket at the start

Secret:

You need two identical packs of cards. Remove two jacks, two queens and one king — all hearts. Glue one queen to one jack back to back — this is your fake card. Put the genuine jack in your pocket unknown to the audience. Show everyone the king, genuine queen and fake card (with the jack side facing them). Put them in a box after you have shown that it is empty. Remove the king and put it in your pocket. Remove the fake card, turned to show the queen side and put that in your pocket also. (Both cards are beside the genuine jack placed there secretly.)

Say, 'The king and queen have left the palace. Who is left there?' They will say 'The jack'. Remove the genuine queen, show the box empty, and remove the genuine jack from your pocket. Explain, 'The queen of hearts made some tarts. She didn't trust jack so she changed places with him by magic.'

If you haven't got two packs of cards cut four rectangles of card and draw simple pictures to represent the jack, queen and king. You can't draw? Write the words *queen*, *king* and *jack* on card. If you do this there is no need to glue two cards — simply write *jack* on one side of the fake card and *queen* on the other.

I'll Read Your Mind

What the audience see:

Four slips of paper are shown. Each has a name on it: BOB, EMMA, JASON, ANGELA. The performer puts the names in four envelopes and places them on a table. Someone chooses a name but tells no one which one she has thought of.

The magician taps the envelopes and the helper silently spells her chosen name — one letter for each tap. When the last letter is tapped the helper says, 'stop'. Opening the envelope she discovers her chosen name inside.

Secret:

Place the envelopes in this order:

Bob	Emma
Jason	Angela

Touch any envelope you like for the first two taps. Then continue in this order until stopped: third tap, BOB; fourth tap, EMMA; fifth tap, JASON; sixth tap, ANGELA. The trick works automatically because each name has the same number of letters as the number of the tap.

Cut And Restored Tape Measure

What the audience see:

The performer shows an envelope and a plastic tape measure. The short ends of the envelope have been cut off. He slides the envelope on to the tape measure. Then he cuts through the centre of the envelope. On pulling the ends of the envelope apart the spectators see that the tape measure is unharmed.

Secret:

You need to prepare a long envelope. If it has a flap on the long side, seal it and cut off the two short edges. If the flap is on the short side, cut it off and cut the other short end, fig 1.

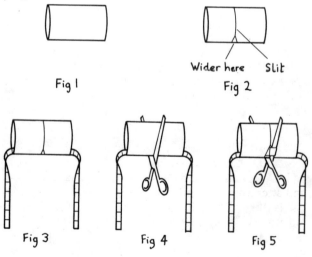

Fig 1

Wider here   Slit

Fig 2

Fig 3   Fig 4   Fig 5

Cut a secret slit across the middle of the address side, fig 2. Widen the slit at the bottom to enable the scissors to be easily inserted.

When you perform the trick, hold the envelope with the slit facing you. Press the edges to make the envelope bulge into a tube shape. Slide the tape measure through so its ends hang down an almost equal amount, fig 3. Insert the scissors into the widened bottom part of the slit. Pass them up and *under* the tape measure and out through the top end of the slit (audience's view, fig 4. Your view, fig 5.) Thus when you cut the envelope the tape measure will be unharmed.

Choice Discovery

What the audience see:

This is a trick where you apparently read somebody's mind in advance. The audience are told that you have written a prediction and it is on the mantelpiece. Someone is asked to choose a colour from red, blue or yellow. Say they select red. You take a piece of paper from under a vase on the mantelpiece. On it is written 'You will choose red'.

Secret:

Write three separate predictions on three pieces of paper. One says, 'You will choose red', the second reads, 'You will choose blue', the third says, 'You will choose yellow'. Fold them and place under three separate objects so that they can't be seen. You merely remember where each predicted colour is and remove the correct paper.

It is essential that the spectators know that you do not use a confederate. To prove this, ask them to toss a table tennis ball to one another. You turn your back as this is being done and after a few seconds call 'stop'. The person holding the ball is the one to help you. If there is no mantelpiece use a radiator shelf or sideboard and put several objects on it under three of which you can hide your predictions. You can, of course, use celebrities or objects instead of colours.

Little Bo Peep

What the audience see:

The performer places four jacks on the table. They represent Bo Peep's sheep. He deals three cards on top of each sheep. One of the piles of cards is selected. The other piles are placed in the pack. The sheep are found in the selected pile.

The Secret:

Three cards (any cards) are hidden behind a box on your table, faces up. Take the four jacks from the pack of cards, show them to the audience and say, 'Let's pretend the jacks are Bo Peep's sheep.' Deal the jacks face up on top of the hidden cards, then pick up the box and show it. 'This is to stand the cards against,' you explain putting the box down again. Next you pick up all seven cards and replace them on top of the pack.

Place the top four cards in a row leaning against the box, backs to the audience fig 1. They will be three different cards and one jack. Tell the audience you are placing the sheep there. Now place the next three cards on the jack (card 1 in fig 1) backs facing the audience again. This pile now has all the jacks in it. Place three more cards on each of the other piles, backs out as before.

Ask someone to indicate two of the piles of cards. If you write numbers along the top of the box it will facilitate matters. If they indicate the jack pile as one of them, remove two *other* piles and put them in the pack. If not, remove the piles selected and put them in the pack. Ask another person to indicate one of the piles left. If the jack pile is selected say, 'I'll use that pile.' If not, remove the selected pile and put it in the pack.

As you have gathered, the spectators have no choice at all. You 'guide' the selections to the pile of cards you want.

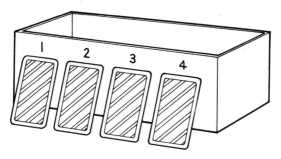

Tell your audience that Bo Peep's sheep are scattered — one in the selected pile of cards and the others in the pack. Ask someone to see whether they can find the sheep in the pack. As they are looking, in vain, turn the jacks round and place them in front of the box. 'Our sheep found their way home just as they did in the nursery rhyme,' you say.

Clairvoyance

What the audience see:

The 'clairvoyant' leaves the room. While she is outside the spectators choose an object in the room. When she returns she is blindfolded. Her partner says, 'We have selected something in this room, can you tell us what it is? Was it the clock?' 'No.' 'Was it the video?' 'No.' 'Was it this chair' 'No.' 'Was it that lamp?' 'Yes'.

She is correct!

The secret:

The word 'that' precedes the chosen object. All the other objects are preceded by words like 'this' or 'the'. Don't repeat this stunt too often — someone may get a clue to the code word. A good way to throw them off the scent is to vary your code. Here is a silent code. For this one the partner merely points to various objects and the clairvoyant tells him when the chosen one has been indicated. In this case the partner points to a red object immediately before the chosen one.

Another way is to point to a selected *number* of objects before the selected one. Perform all three codes one after the other and you'll baffle the most observant of your audience.

Happy Birthday

What the audience see:

A sheet of paper is put on the table. A few strips of paper are placed on the sheet. The latter is folded around the pieces of paper. When unfolded the strips have formed themselves into the words HAPPY BIRTHDAY.

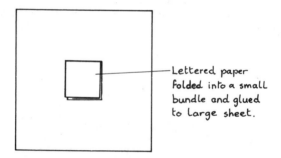

Lettered paper folded into a small bundle and glued to large sheet.

The secret:

You need two sheets of a dark-coloured paper and some paper of a contrasting light colour. Let's assume you are using black and yellow. Cut out the letters HAPPY BIRTH-DAY from the yellow paper and glue them to one of the black sheets. Put a dab of glue in the centre of the unprepared black sheet and stick it to the back of the lettered sheet. Fold the lettered paper into a small bundle, fig 1. Cut a few strips of yellow paper and you are all set to perform the trick.

Hold the black paper by the top corners so the bundle is hidden behind it. Place it on your table. Show the yellow strips and place them on the black sheet. Fold it over the strips so it makes a bundle the size of the hidden one. Pick it up in one hand and wave the magic wand over it with your other hand. It is an easy matter to turn the bundle over as you get rid of your wand. Open the paper to reveal the birthday message taking care not to expose the bundle on the rear.

A small nick with scissors will assist you to locate the top of the message sheet so you don't unfold it upside-down!

Vanishing Coin

What the audience see:

The magician puts a handkerchief over his hand. He shows a coin and places it in the centre of the handkerchief. Taking a corner of the handkerchief in his other hand he flicks it up. The coin has disappeared.

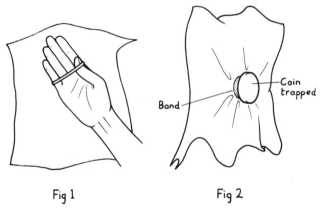

Fig 1   Fig 2

Secret:

Unknown to the audience a rubber band is placed over your thumb and fingers, hidden by the handkerchief. As you flick the handkerchief, release the band from your fingers and thumb. It traps the coin in the handkerchief. The diagrams will make it clear.

Noah's Magic Animals

What the audience see:

Ten matches are shown. The magician picks up two in each hand alternately until they are all in his hands. He puts six matches down on the table again in alternate pairs. On opening his hands the audience see four matches in his right hand while his left hand is empty.

The secret:

Tell your audience about Noah and his ark. 'Let's pretend these matches are some of the animals. There are ten altogether. As you know, the animals went into the ark in pairs.'

You take two matches into your right hand, two into your left hand, two into your right hand, two into your left hand and two into your right hand. You now have four matches in the left hand and six in the right.

'Now let's put six of the animals into the ark,' you say, placing alternate pairs down on the table. This time you commence with the *left hand*, putting two from the left hand, two from the right and so on. The trick is done. Tell your audience, 'There are two animals in each hand. They played a joke on old Noah. When he went to feed them he discovered there were none here and four here.' Open your hands so everyone can see what you say is true.

If you want to enhance the mystery, ask someone to choose one of your hands — left or right. If they indicate the right hand say, 'I'll make the animals appear in the hand you chose.' If they say, 'Left hand' tell them, 'I'll make them vanish from my left hand and appear in my right hand.'

Paper Tearing

What the audience see:

The performer shows a sheet of paper. He folds it a few times and tears pieces off. Unfolding the paper his audience see a ship's wheel pattern.

How to do it:

Fold the paper in half, fig 1. Then in half again, fig 2. Turn corner A over to B, fig 3. Then fold CD to CE, fig 4. Tear away shaded parts and unfold to reveal the wheel. It will help if you pre-fold the paper and mark the shaded pattern with pencil to guide you. Other patterns can be made using the same folds.

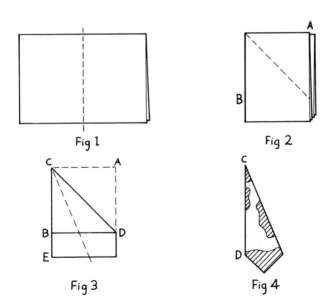

Fig 1

Fig 2

Fig 3

Fig 4

Party Cakes

Candles

Although only certain of the cakes illustrate the use of candles, these may, of course, be wanted on any cake. Of the cakes where they are not specified, they might best be placed on the board, into piped butter icing rosettes in the Robot, Pony and Dragon cakes. Use a number 8 nozzle to pipe the rosettes and ice blue icing (Robot), green or deep pink icing (Pony), and yellow icing (Dragon).

Colourings

Two kinds of food colouring are used in the cakes. These are liquid colours which are bought in bottles, and concentrated colour which is supplied in tubs and which can be bought in some delicatessens and specialist kitchen shops. These are referred to in the recipes as 'colour' for liquid colour, and 'con. colour' for concentrated colour. The exceptions to this are gold and silver colour which comes in powdered form and should be mixed with a little oil before painting on.

The colours of the concentrated colour tend to be very vivid and pure, which is marvellous where a strong colour is needed. Where a pale result is wanted and concentrated colour is specified, be sure to add only a very little at a time until the colour you need is reached. A good example of this is in the use of Paprika concentrated colour. To make a skin tone only the merest hint is needed. Where colour is painted on, a fine soft brush should be used. For painting on eyes and mouths use a brush with a very fine tip.

Fondant Icing

There are on the market very good ready-to-use fondant icings, and using these may well be considered the simpler and quicker procedure. If you prefer to make your own fondant, however, a recipe is given in the Recipe section. Whichever is preferred, its use and application are the same.

Colouring Fondant

When adding colour to fondant or marzipan be sure to mix thoroughly, initially with a wooden spoon and then kneading until the colour is thoroughly incorporated.

Rolling Out Fondant

It will be seen that the instructions in the recipes require simply that the fondant is rolled out. A sufficient thickness in almost all cases would be just less than 6 mm/¼ inch. When rolling both fondant and marzipan, dust the work surface and rolling pin with icing sugar to prevent sticking, and continue to do so as necessary while you work.

Hardening Fondant

It is sometimes recommended that sections of fondant are left to harden completely before assembling or placing in position. This can lead to cracking, however, and I prefer to use the fondant while still pliable. Modelled pieces of fondant should be placed on to non-stick paper which has been dusted lightly with icing sugar, whether they are to be left to harden or are simply being assembled before being used.

Applying Fondant

Small pieces of fondant can be picked up as they are and applied as specified in the instructions. Large pieces, however, are heavy, and to avoid them stretching out of shape they should be eased over a rolling pin and lifted with the rolling pin taking some of the weight. Care should be taken not to stretch the fondant as it is applied. The area of cake to be covered should first be brushed with sieved apricot jam, using a pastry brush. The fondant will then adhere easily. Where a fondant piece is applied to a fondant surface, egg white, beaten lightly with a fork to break up the albumen, should be used instead of jam as it will not show.

Preparation of Tins, Cooling and Cutting

All non-stick tins must be greased before use. If the sandwich tins used are the kind with a bar that turns around the base, then these need only be greased. Otherwise they need to be lined with greased greaseproof paper as described below. All other tins and containers, including food tins, loaf tins and basins, need to be lined in this way. First cut pieces of greaseproof paper to fit the container. Lightly grease the container and line with paper, then grease the paper.

When the cake is baked, leave for a few minutes before turning on to a wire rack to cool. This is especially important where the cake is a large one. Peel the paper off while the cake is still warm.

All trimming and cutting is done when the cakes are quite cool, otherwise a clean line will not be achieved. Use a serrated knife as this will give the cleanest edge.

The Recipes

Victoria Sponge

	Metric	Imperial	American
Margarine or butter	350 g	12 oz	1½ cups
Castor sugar	350 g	12 oz	1½ cups
Eggs	6	6	6
Self-raising flour	350 g	12 oz	3 cups
Baking powder	1 tsp	1 tsp	1 tsp
Milk			

Cream the fat and sugar until light. Sift the flour and baking powder together. Whisk the eggs and add alternately to the creamed ingredients with the sifted flour, beating well after each addition. Add milk as necessary to give a dropping consistency. Bake at 190°C/375°F/Mark 5 until the cake is springy to the touch (test the centre) and has started to shrink from the sides of the tin. With a large cake be sure to leave it long enough for the centre to be cooked.

This basic recipe can be varied by adding finely grated orange or lemon rind or flavouring essences. The quantities given here are for a 6-egg mixture. Whatever the quantity given for a particular cake, however, the proportions remain the same. Thus a 5-egg mixture would use 275 g/10 oz each of sugar, fat and flour, an 8-egg mixture would use 450 g/1 lb each.

Light Fatless Sponge

	Metric	Imperial	American
Eggs	6	6	6
Castor sugar	225 g	8 oz	1 cup
Plain flour	225 g	8 oz	2 cups
Hot water	30 ml	2 tbsp	2 tbsp

Sift the flour. Whisk the eggs and sugar in a bowl over a pan of hot water until light and creamy. The mixture should be quite thick. Remove the bowl from the heat and whisk until cool. Fold in half the sifted flour using a metal spoon. Fold in the remaining flour in the same way and add the hot water, stirring lightly. Pour the mixture into the prepared tin (see p. 108) and tip the tin to allow the mixture fully to cover the surface. Bake at 220°C/425°F/Mark 7 for about 10–15 minutes until risen and golden brown. Turn out onto wire rack to cool.

Butter Icing

This is made by adding sifted icing sugar gradually to creamed butter or margarine, moistening with milk to give a good spreading consistency. The quantities given in the instructions refer to the amount of fat used, with 1½–2 times this weight being added in icing sugar. Thus a quantity given as 225 g/8 oz butter icing requires 225 g/8 oz butter or margarine and 350–450 g/12 oz–1 lb icing sugar. If liquid colour is to be used and the colour needed is a strong one, take account of this when making up the butter icing and make it a little stiffer than otherwise. More milk can always be added after the desired colour has been achieved.

It is a good idea to secure all the cakes to the boards with butter icing. This will keep them firmly to the board while being worked on.

Fondant Icing

	Metric	Imperial	American
Egg white	1	1	1
Icing sugar	450 g	1 lb	3 cups
Liquid glucose	30 ml	2 tbsp	2 tbsp

Add the sieved icing sugar and the warmed liquid glucose to the egg white gradually, until the required consistency is obtained. The fondant should be pliable but firm. If it is too stiff add more egg white; if it is not stiff enough, add more icing sugar. When not being used, fondant should be wrapped in cling film and stored in an airtight container at room temperature. Do not keep it in the refrigerator.

Glacé Icing

This is made by adding warm water to sifted icing sugar until the required consistency is reached. The icing should be at least thick enough to coat the back of a spoon. Add the water very gradually as very little is needed. 50–75 g/2–3 oz icing sugar will need only 7–15 ml/½–1 tbsp water.

Robot

Ingredients

1.5 kg/3 lb 4 oz fondant
50 g/2 oz butter icing
300 g/10 oz glacé icing
Ice blue con colour
Silver lustre colour
Silver balls
Jelly sweets
Sieved apricot jam
Egg white

Equipment

Nos. 2 and 8 nozzles
Piping bag
Fine paintbrush
900 ml/2 pint basin
Four 23 cm/7 in round
sandwich tins
15 × 7 cm/6 × 3 in
rectangular tin
Pastry brush

1 Bake a 12-egg sponge mixture in the sandwich tins, basin and loaf tin, filling the latter only half full. Trim all tops flat. Sandwiching together with butter icing, layer round sponges in centre of board, with upturned basin cake on top. Cut loaf cake in half lengthwise.

2 Roll out 1 kg/2 lb white fondant. Measure height and circumference of cake and cut a rectangle to fit the round cakes, a curved strip for the dome and a circle for the top. Brush cake with jam and apply, using a rolling pin to lift fondant.

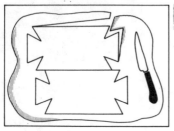

3 Roll 225 g/8 oz white fondant and cut shapes to cover the two oblong pieces as illustrated. Brush these with jam and apply fondant.

4 Place oblongs on board at each side of robot body. Roll 100 g/4 oz white fondant about 2.5 cm/1 in thick and cut two pieces 4 cm/1½ in wide and 10 cm/4 in long. Slightly flatten and round one end and make patterns with the handle of a teaspoon and the flat blade of a knife. Attach to robot with egg white rounded end at the top.

5 Colour 225 g/8 oz fondant blue and roll out. Cut twelve shapes for top of robot as illustrated, six of each kind. Cut two strips to go round robot, 2.5 cm/1 in wide and 1 cm/½ in wide, squares for the ends of feet and arch shapes to fit into recesses on legs. Attach with egg white.

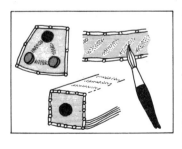

6 With glacé icing and no. 2 nozzle pipe round all blue shapes. Place silver balls in piping round all pieces. Attach jelly lights to top pieces with egg white. Mix silver colouring into a paste with a little oil and paint lines on top panels, lower band and top of feet. Using no. 8 nozzle and 50 g/2 oz blue butter icing pipe rosettes along base of robot and a line along base of feet.

113

Fire-Breathing Dragon

Ingredients

975 g/2 lb 3 oz fondant
75 g/3 oz butter icing
Green colour
Egg yellow con colour
Grape violet con colour
Black colour
15 g/½ oz Sugar (granulated or castor)
Sieved apricot jam
Egg white

Equipment

Nos. 2, 3 and 8 nozzles
Piping bag
Pastry brush
20 cm/8 in round sandwich tin
900 g/2 lb loaf tin
35 cm/14 in round board
Non-stick paper

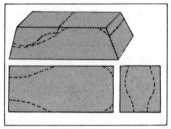

1 Bake a 6-egg sponge mixture in the loaf tin and sandwich tin. Trim loaf cake flat and turn over. Cut loaf cake horizontally as shown to give outline of body. Then make vertical cuts on body section, rounding back end. Cut head from remaining section as illustrated.

2 From round cake cut two tail sections and back haunches and feet as illustrated. Cut back haunches section in half horizontally to make two.

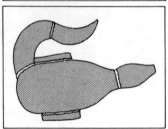

3 Assemble dragon on board, positioning body to one side to allow room for tail and joining pieces with butter icing. Turn the end section of tail over so that the tail curves as an 'S' shape.

114

4 Colour 700 g/1½ lb fondant green. Roll out and cut shapes for head and haunches as shown. Score all over with lines using a knife. Brush cake with jam and apply. Cut two small triangles for ears and position on head, securing with egg white.

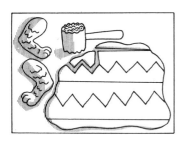

5 Cut strips of scales from remaining rolled fondant. If wished, a meat tenderiser can be used to texture the surface before cutting the scales. Use trimmings of green fondant to roll and shape two forelegs as shown, scoring surface with a knife.

6 Brush tail and uncovered area of body with jam and cover with scales starting at end of tail and working towards head, overlapping layers slightly. Using the handle of a teaspoon, pull fondant into folds above and below eye area.

7 Colour 50 g/2 oz fondant purple and roll out. Cut about 16 spines grading from 12 mm/½ in to 3 cm/1¼ in high. Score with vertical lines. Cut snout from purple fondant and make two holes with the end of a straw. With the back of a knife make an indented line down the centre to take the 'fire'. Make six teeth about 12 mm/½ in long and six claws from scraps of white fondant.

8 Attach spines with egg white along back and tail placing largest in the centre of back and the smaller each side, ending with the smallest towards the tip of the tail. Colour a scrap of fondant yellow and make flat round eyes, indenting a line across centre. Fix a thin roll of purple fondant in this line. Position eyes, teeth and claws as illustrated, securing all features with egg white.

9 Colour 75 g/3 oz butter icing yellow and using no. 3 nozzle pipe dots along join of scales to head and along top of haunches. Using no. 2 nozzle, outline scales with yellow and pipe line where snout joins head.

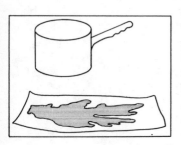

10 Colour 125 g/4 oz fondant dark grey and 125g /4 oz light grey. Chop when beginning to dry. Brush board with jam and cover with 'stones'. Dissolve 15 g/½ oz sugar in 1 tablespoon water and boil without stirring until a caramel colour. Pour spoonfuls into long shapes on non-stick paper and allow to set. Use the best shape as 'flames' from dragon's mouth.

Pony

Ingredients

575 g/1 lb 4 oz butter icing
50 g/2 oz fondant
Grape violet con. colour
Pink colour
Green colour
Liquorice Allsort
Egg white

Equipment

No. 8 nozzle
Piping bag
900 g/2 lb loaf tin
450 g/1 lb loaf tin
25 cm/10 in round board

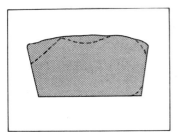

1 Bake a 6-egg sponge mixture in the two loaf tins. From larger cake cut shape for main body as illustrated, making horizontal cut first, then vertical.

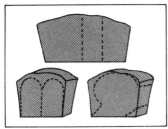

2 Cut small cake in half across its width. Cut one section in half again. From one quarter section cut one hind leg and from the other cut two forelegs as illustrated.

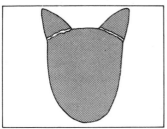

3 From the remaining half of the small block cut the head and ears as illustrated, making vertical cut for head first, then horizontal.

4 Assemble pony on board joining all pieces with butter icing. Cut the second hind leg from a left-over piece of sponge and place in position. Colour 350 g/12 oz butter icing pale mauve and cover cake entirely, smoothing surface.

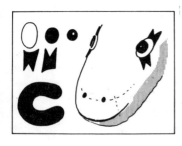

5 Incise mouth with a knife and nostrils with the end of a skewer. Make the eyes. Cut two circles and four shapes from a black round liquorice allsort as shown. Make two circles from purple fondant and two small dots of white fondant. Join pieces together with egg white and press into position on pony. Make horseshoe from purple fondant and position on tucked under back leg as shown.

6 Colour 50 g/2 oz butter icing green. Spread on board and cover with 125 g/4 oz shredded coconut coloured green. Colour 175 g/6 oz butter icing pink and using no. 8 nozzle pipe a flowing mane and tail.

7 From 25–50 g/1–2 oz white fondant make flowers. Roll into a ball and press to flatten. Pull in edges with the back of a knife to make petals. Attach three tiny yellow fondant balls to centre of flowers with egg white. Place flowers in position on pony and in mane and tail.

Toy Bear

Ingredients

400 g/15 oz butter icing
100 g/4 oz fondant
Egg yellow con. colour
Green colour
Blue colour
Chocolate brown colour
Liquorice Allsort
Egg white

Equipment

No. 8 nozzle
Piping bag
23 × 18 cm/9 × 7 in
rectangular tin
18 cm/7 in round sandwich tin
23 cm/9 in round board
Candles

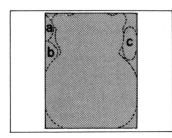

1 Bake a 7-egg sponge mixture in the rectangular and round tins. From rectangle cut out main body shape and pieces for the back of the head (a), nose (b) and cheeks (c).

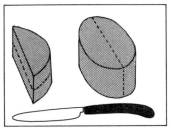

2 Cut piece 'a' horizontally to make two pieces for the back of the head and piece 'c' vertically to make two cheek pieces.

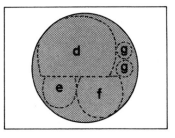

3 Cut the round cake as illustrated. The pieces will be used for the back of the bear (d) and (e), the tummy (f) and feet (g).

119

4 Assemble the front of the bear as illustrated while cake is still lying flat. Joining all pieces with butter icing, use piece 'f' on body and pieces 'c' and 'b' on face.

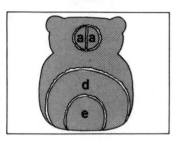

5 Stand bear up and secure to board with butter icing. Assemble back of bear using pieces 'd' and 'e' on body and 'a' on head and joining all pieces with butter icing.

6 Put feet (g) in position and trim edges on cake where necessary to give a rounded effect. Colour 375 g/14 oz butter icing yellow and cover bear entirely, moulding the shape of arms as you do so. Roughen surface all over with a fork.

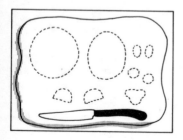

7 Roll 100 g/4 oz white fondant and cut shapes for tummy, face, feet, ears, eyes and nose as illustrated. Position face, ears and feet on bear.

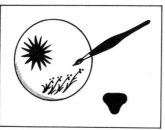

8 Using yellow, green and blue colouring and a fine brush, paint picture on fondant tummy. Paint nose piece yellow. Allow to dry. Position on bear, fixing nose to face with egg white. Using no. 8 nozzle and the remaining butter icing coloured blue, pipe rosettes on board for the number of candles required and place a candle on each.

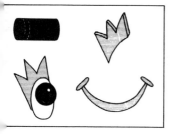

9 Make eyes and mouth. Cut shapes as illustrated and roll a mouth from brown fondant. Cut two slices from a black round liquorice allsort. Assemble eyes as shown, putting a small dot of white fondant on the black. Join all pieces with egg white and secure in position in the same way.

Swag Bag Ideas

Children of all ages enjoy receiving a party bag of tricks and treats to take home. A piece of cake, sweets and balloons are a must. Here are some suggestions that should meet the approval of your guests.

For The Girls

- [ ] Cake
- [ ] Sweets
- [ ] Balloon
- [ ] Plastic jewellery
- [ ] Hair band
- [ ] Pencil sharpener
- [ ] Pencils
- [ ] Mini-games

- [ ] Cake
- [ ] Sweets
- [ ] Balloon

- [ ] Bubbles
- [ ] Paint brush
- [ ] Watercolours
- [ ] Streamers
- [ ] Dot-to-dot pictures

For The Boys

- [ ] Cake
- [ ] Sweets
- [ ] Balloon
- [ ] Small ball
- [ ] Model truck
- [ ] Funny nose
- [ ] Whistle
- [ ] Stickers

- [ ] Cake
- [ ] Sweets
- [ ] Balloon
- [ ] Badges

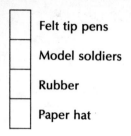

Felt tip pens

Model soldiers

Rubber

Paper hat

Checklist: Swag Bag Shopping List

- [ ] Sweets
- [ ] Cake boxes
- [ ] Balloons
- [ ] Streamers
- [ ] Whistles
- [ ] Mini-games
- [ ] Rubber
- [ ] Pencils
- [ ] Pencil sharpeners
- [ ] Stickers
- [ ] Crayons
- [ ] Felt tip pens
- [ ] Jotting pad
- [ ] Diary
- [ ] Bubbles
- [ ] Plastic jewellery
- [ ] Paint brush
- [ ] Watercolour paints

- [ ] Funny nose and ears
- [ ] Small ruler
- [ ] Model car/truck
- [ ] Model animals/soldiers
- [ ] Hair band
- [ ] Small ball
- [ ] Badges
- [ ] Scrap book
- [ ] Party bags
- [ ] Ribbon
- [ ] Name tags

Party Game Index